The Secular Faith C

C000233398

ISSUES IN CONTEMPORARY RELIGION

Series editors: Christopher Lamb and M. Darrol Bryant

The volumes in this series are interdisciplinary and present their subjects from global and cross-religious perspectives, examining issues that cut across traditions and emerge in distinctive ways in different religions and cultural settings. Based on sound scholarship, the books are intended for undergraduate courses and for professionals involved in inter-faith dialogue.

Also available in the series:

Dan Cohn-Sherbok, *Understanding the Holocaust: An Introduction*

Christopher Lamb and M. Darrol Bryant (eds),
Religious Conversion: Contemporary Practices and Controversies

George D. Chryssides, *Exploring New Religions*

Clive and Jane Erricker (eds),
Contemporary Spiritualities: Social and Religious Contexts

The Secular Faith Controversy

Religion in Three Dimensions

Edward Bailey

CONTINUUM
London and New York

Continuum
The Tower Building, 11 York Road, London SE1 7NX
370 Lexington Avenue, New York, NY 10017-6503

First published 2001

© Edward Bailey 2001

All rights reserved. No part of this publication may be reproduced or transmitted in
any form or by any means, electronic or mechanical, including photocopying,
recording or any information storage or retrieval system, without permission in
writing from the publishers.

British Library Cataloguing in Publication Data
A catalogue record for this book is available from the British Library.

ISBN 0-8264-4924-7 (hardback)
 0-8264-4925-5 (paperback)

Library of Congress Cataloging-in-Publication Data
Bailey, Edward I. (Edward Ian)
    The secular faith controversy : religion in three dimensions / Edward Bailey.
        p.   cm. — (Issues in contemporary religion)
    Includes biographical references and index.
    ISBN 0-8264-4924-7 — ISBN 0-8264-4925-5 (pbk.)
    1. Secularization (Theology)   I. Title.   II. Series.

    BT83.7.B35   2001
    200—dc21   2001017323

Typeset by BookEns Ltd, Royston, Herts.
Printed and bound in Great Britain by Biddles Ltd., Guildford and King's Lynn

Contents

CONTENTS

Preface

A short volume, such as this, might be expected to be coherent and point to a single practical proposal. This volume is united by two different themes: the attempt to look at some religious practicalities (as experienced by the incumbent of a Church of England parish) in the light of some degree of acquaintance with Religious Studies, and the attempt to look at Religious Studies (largely as experienced through the pursuit of 'implicit religion') in the light of parochial and extra-parochial experience. Although there are reasons for thinking that the time may be ripe for bridging this gap between practice and theory, this book is less a programme than a collection of comments and suggested hypotheses offered in the hope of encouraging a process.

Worked and reworked, while particularly involved with both ecclesiastical and academic developments, it has gradually been grown but, when finalized, it will always omit some things one wanted to say. Writing and rewriting on the run, so to speak, has been more than usually trying, not only for the Series Editor and the publisher's representatives (Christopher Lamb and Janet Joyce and assistants) but for Diane Rix, yet again, trying to produce that 'final' manuscript. I would particularly like to thank her for her perseverance and the others for their patience.

Edward Bailey
26 October 2000

Introduction: A model of society, consciousness and religion

The Middle Ages, as the name suggests, were only so called when a later age felt that classical learning had been successfully recovered. If they called themselves anything, it was probably not a 'historical' name. Other periods, such as the Renaissance and Reformation, saw themselves as having a particular theme. In the case of the Enlightenment, it effectively described the vocation of a chosen people with an implied mission statement for human history as a whole.

Briefer periods may afterwards be seen as pre-war, post-war or inter-war. A particular decade such as the 1890s may describe itself as *fin-de-siècle*, while the last decade of the following century tried to see itself as bravely entering a new millennium. The 1830s saw themselves in apocalyptic terms and there were similar tinges in the 1970s.

The decade of the 1960s saw itself as a hinge between two worlds, which we have subsequently learned to call 'modernism' and 'post-modernism'. Naturally, there is room for journalistic and scholarly debate regarding their characteristics, causes and core (and exact title) but few dispute that a change of culture, of greater significance than the changes in the decades immediately before or after, took place in the Western world then. Indeed, 1968 has become a shorthand symbol in its own right.

One of the signs that an age was ending was the fascination, on the part of religious people, with secularization. In part it was an acknowledgement that a new world had been born: that it was as impossible to reconstitute the medieval Church in the present day as the *ancien régime,* although both had been attempted in theology and liturgy, spirituality and architecture during the nineteenth century. In part it was a recovered recognition that divinity was both mundane and cosmic, as well as ecclesiastical: it didn't need to have an initial capital letter, let alone be focused into a 'God', as the transcendent was immanent. In part it marked a coming of age for the social sciences, whose students were at the forefront of the events that gave 1968 its symbolic significance (Martin, 1968).

So intoxicated were some theologians and clergy with the prospective realization of total secularization, that it needed sociologists who were themselves religious, such as David Martin (1969) and Andrew Greeley (1973), to remind them that religion was a great survivor and that secularization (which had no agreed definition), far from being an inevitable, universal and irreversible law, was an unproven hypothesis.

Hindsight suggests that Christian espousal of the thesis indicated, first, that the doctrine of secularization found a natural home within the Christian worldview and, therefore, might not be so easily accommodated by other worldviews or praxis and, second, that the articulation of what, for a hundred years, had largely been an assumption on the part of the social sciences was to throw down a gauntlet which might become a boomerang. Harvey Cox's discussion of 'exorcism' in the secular city (1965) showed *en passant* how 'secularity' could backfire into a spirituality that was both traditional and relevant.

By the 1970s it was clear that a new age had begun. Sanskritization (Srinivas, 1952) showed that the thesis of secularization was not universally applicable. Power politics increasingly indicated the reversibility of any such trend. An international sociology of religion (*Journal of Oriental Studies*, 1987) suggested it was culturally, if not religiously (or even theologically), specific. The import of 'foreign' religions, the development of new ones and the reinvention of ancient traditions indicated the incomplete character of secularization, even in its missionary heartlands. The concept remains relevant but the eschatological note of the 1960s took on the 'gloaming' appearance of an Indian summer, a secular interlude before a religious storm.

The acceptability of certain concepts can be charted quite precisely (Dicey, 1893), particularly with the development of rapid, formal, mass communication. Examples are violent and sexual behaviours: battered wives, babies and old people and – likewise in chronological sequence – homosexuality, incest, paedophilia. A parallel development can be seen in the use of some formerly religious terms outside their earlier ecclesiastical context: 'pastoral' in the 1960s in psychology and education, 'supernatural' in the 1970s in marketing and popular journals, and 'spiritual' in the 1980s – everywhere but above all, perhaps, in the worlds of education, health and work.

How to understand the new situation is not immediately obvious. That we need to understand it, both for practical purposes and in order to understand ourselves, is clear. That, with the odd exceptions ('swan songs'), the secularization thesis arouses little overt controversy at present suggests that this is a good moment to articulate a new model which may find widespread agreement. What were seen as belonging to two separate worlds ('secular' and 'faith') can now be seen as belonging together, like two sides of the same coin. Rather than promoting a contest between them, we may want to use them as complementary currencies within the larger 'economy' of human life, ideas and consciousness.

The model of consciousness and religious experience, which is suggested in the following pages and set out in the Appendix, may be briefly sketched at this point.

It starts with a threefold typology of society: the customary division into the small-scale, the historical and the contemporary. In order to avoid any suspicion of projecting our experience of society either 'backwards' or 'forwards', however, it considers that the successive trio of 'social' types would more accurately be characterized if they were described as ecological, social and cultural.

Next, it describes the form of consciousness in these three settings as characterized respectively by an intensification and consequent bifurcation of consciousness, by increasing individuation and hence the potential for interrelating, and by a burgeoning conscientization and a balancing contextualization.

The content of religious experience in these situations can be described respectively as the sacred, the holy and the human. The character of the relationship with that content changes from one of sensing, to encounter, to commitment. Thus the core of religious experience could be described as changing from a fear of divinity (awe), to praise of God (a personal Being), to joining with GOD (the unknowable Absolute). The expression of human relationships can likewise be characterized as changing from, for instance, 'My darling' (an expletive descriptive of an emotional attitude), to the use of a personal name (e.g. John), to the use of a number. So the nature, character or meaning of being 'personal' changes in the three types of context, as does the nature, character or meaning of 'religious' – and the nature, character or meaning of 'society'.

Finally, however, it is suggested that the model, with its historical penumbra, is a myth, which is designed to facilitate the coordination of various concepts and hypotheses. It is intended to be of value to those who are more interested in the practise, leadership or study of religion (as indicated by the divisions within each of the first three chapters) than in its historical development. So it is of practical application, first, to the development of the individual and, second, to the social experience and consciousness and, therefore, potential religiosity of everyday life.

For, on the one hand, most individuals begin life in a small-scale society (or ecology), archetypically on mother's knee (and are addressed as 'Darling', etc.), before moving on to the differentiated, role-bearing, literate or 'historical society' of the primary school (where they are known by an individual name) and then graduating into the 'contemporary culture' of the Saturday job (and of identity by bar-code). And, on the other hand, each individual (assuming they participate in the third stage at all) moves between the three types of social experience, and ways of being a person, on most days of their life.

Some such balance between, first, intimacy, second, teamwork and, third, anonymity may also be considered advisable for the sake of psychic health, if these ways of being a person have once been divided. In which case, it may be suggested that the total spectrum of people's mental, religious and spiritual experience can, could or should be expected to be equally diverse. Properly understood, it may already run the gamut of sensing a cosmic sacred, encountering a personal holy and commitment to an ineffable quality of humanness, consciously or unconsciously, in some degree, daily. This, then, is the *particular* reference of the 'three dimensions' of the volume's subtitle.

Part I
The religious situation in three dimensions

1. Problems

Prelude: common misconceptions and three groups

On Wednesday 11 November 1992, the General Synod of the Church of England decided to enable women to be ordained as priests. The incident and, in the present context in particular, its reporting and the reaction to it are significant because they illustrate a number of functional issues in contemporary religion in an event of a very public nature.

To my surprise, it was headlined in that night's North American *CN News*. Next morning it was front-page news (second only to the new President's laryngitis) in the relatively provincial paper of Burlington, Vermont. Fellow attenders at a pair of large academic gatherings, concerned with the sociology of religion and with the study of religion generally (the Society for the Scientific Study of Religion and the American Academy of Religion), raised it with me as often as they asked about the effects of the Prince of Wales' divorce upon the Church of England. If their questions revealed the limits of their knowledge of the empirical realities of Church life in England, my surprise at their questions revealed the limits of my own awareness, even via friends of long standing, of where they (American academics) were 'at' or 'coming from'.

Winston Churchill's aphorism about Britain and America being 'divided by a common language' refers to more than merely accent. It has practical consequences. For instance, 'Evangelicals' in Britain not only assume that the epithet carries the same resonances in North America but also envisage religion occupying a similar space in the social and cultural structure of the United States. Likewise, some of those in Britain who see themselves as Catholic (either Roman Catholic or Anglican) and tend to look to the European mainland, nevertheless avert their gaze from, for example, the

Church in France and all that is not as confrontational as themselves. The essence of the difference can be seen in whether we describe such positions adjectivally, simply as evangelical and catholic, or whether we identify the people substantively, as 'Evangelicals' or 'Catholics'.

Academically, in other words, sociology and psychology may be germane for understanding the form of religion in North America, but in Europe social and cultural anthropology, including the anthropology of religion, are more relevant to the mode that religion takes. However, it is doubtful whether the curricula, either of the academic study of religion or of preparation for professional ministry, have adequately recognized this. Such a viewpoint can itself, of course, be contextualized as peculiarly Anglican, English and parochial and valued, or dismissed, as 'peculiar' in the traditional sense or in the pejorative one – but Jenkins (1999) may be a harbinger of change.

Similarly, relationships between religion and the State are as varied, even in such cognate countries as the UK and the USA, as they are complex, historical in origin and nuanced. I recall my own surprise in the 1970s and 1980s upon discovering, first, that some European governments actually collect taxes for the Churches (who also fulfil, however, some of the administrative and welfare functions of the State, as Britain would see it) and, second, that such an avowedly secular state as France could pay for the repair of churches (and church organs). Indeed, alerted by that double discovery, I now venture to mention whenever North American scholars describe the Church of England as a 'State Church', thinking it to be like some to be found on the continent of Europe, that being 'Established' has not involved any particular financial favours since the grant of a million pounds in 1818 and half a million pounds in 1824 for building new churches. (In the 1990s the government-sponsored English Heritage programme began to recognize some Anglican churches *and other worship buildings* as parts of the nation's *history*, but the total grant towards their repair came to less than the tax paid on those repairs.)

Nor are such misunderstandings restricted to the Atlantic or to the immediately topical. After talking for most of a day in Lund with a leading sociologist of religion (whose data even included the amount given in the 'collection' each Sunday at every parish church in Sweden), I was nonplussed because he was amazed by my mention of a 65-year-old man being confirmed in my parish the previous

Sunday. I learnt that in our near-twin, the Church of Sweden, what each of us calls confirmation happens at 15 or not at all. Conversely, the fact that most Swedes are confirmed but very few indeed attend church afterwards does not mean that the rite is undertaken lightly. On the contrary, even more time and attention are given to preparing candidates for it than in the Church of England.

So frequent are such 'misunderstandings' and so unfortunate are their consequences sometimes that the very term has become a euphemism for 'dispute'. However, even an innocent and genuine *mis-communication* can lead to erroneous information, images and goals. Thus the Church of England's 'parish' means all the residents (not least, but not only, all the baptised, whether or not they attend any church) within an exactly defined geographical area. It is a human community (while recognizing that each of these terms might be seen as relative). However, in North America the 'parish' seems to become, even for the Roman Catholic and Orthodox Churches, either the equivalent of 'congregation' or else of enrolled (or perhaps sacramental) membership of their own denomination.

This too has practical consequences. An essentially Baptist or voluntarist, individualistic and activist understanding of Church membership has been content to measure religiosity by counting the physical bodies at public services on Sundays. By the end of the 1990s it was realized (at last, cp. Bailey, 1976) that many belong to churches without attending either every Sunday or every week (and they are different). Indeed, many at least judge themselves to belong who only attend for family life-events – and most social sciences advocate 'listening to the natives' (Bailey, 1995). In Britain, these simple but misleading criteria (based on simplistic understandings of the phenomena themselves) led to underestimates of the personal and political power of religion, which have then tended to become self-fulfilling. (Ironically, Evangelical statisticians have promulgated the Enlightenment schism between Catholics and *philosophes*!) In the United States a similarly simplistic approach to human behaviour may have encouraged that long-standing inflation of the Sunday churchgoing statistics that seemed to become apparent in the 1990s.

Whenever language and, thus, subjectivity is involved, it is difficult to see how such misunderstandings can ever be totally avoided. 'Church' and 'religion', for instance, like 'father' or 'mother' are bound to mean something different to everyone – and, indeed, to each person at various stages in their lives. The problem is exacerbated, however, when the subjective component is denied; then 'my truth' becomes 'the truth' – and 'your truth' is hardly even seen as true for you. This denial, that the search for truth is both continuous and corporate, could be seen as one of those common strands that sometimes seem to be so elusive in all that we want to call 'fundamentalism'.

Such problems have become notorious in Church history. The Creed as an overall *symbol* lost out to detailed discussions of the historical and metaphysical validity of its individual parts, such as 'substance', 'virgin birth' (usually meaning virginal conception) or the resurrection of the physical (*sic*) 'body'. Likewise, 'the' sacraments, instead of *making* the Church ('we are what we [do and] eat'), tended to become visual aids to assist in the understanding of particular doctrines. In the same way, the philosophy of religion (and even some empirical studies of religion) dismissed 'functional definitions' of religion, not as tautologous (what other sorts could there be?), but as somehow inferior to what they called 'ontological definitions'.

No doubt parallel misunderstandings can be found in other religions than Christianity, in the realm either of practise or of solidarity, if not of 'creed'. They also afflict communication between those with an interest in religion, on the one hand, such as the general public, the religious affairs journalist and the analyst of religion, and, on the other, the religious practitioner and leader.

If the discovery of mutual misinformation was the first point of significance about that 1992 vote, within the present context, the second point has already been indicated: the widespread interest in the News item. For years it had been clear that the mass media in Britain cannot cope with the topic of religion (although in fairness it may also be asked, 'Who can?'). For decades the broadsheets acknowledged its existence simply by reporting ecclesiastical appointments and including a weekly reflection (usually by a cleric); now they have 'progressed' to the manufacture of controversies (which usually involves missing both the real 'successes' and most of the real scandals). Meanwhile the tabloids, as in some Punch-and-Judy-show ritual, can still see only 'toffee-nosed' bishops, wayward 'vicars' and 'bigoted' sects, with the very occasional discovery of one of the 'quiet in the land' (usually in the context of a real or imagined persecution by the religious 'authorities').

Thus, for years it has been known (but ignored) that far more people take part in (organized) religion than, even as spectators, in professional football (and that church magazines, as a genre, have mass circulation figures). For years it has been as clear of the Churches in Britain as of the Church in Russia that something more than mere habit and inertia must keep them going because (as the BBC's Gerald Priestland pointed out in the 1970s) the same little band of 'old women' (whom 'political correctness' somehow allowed to be patronized, if not mocked) could not have been there throughout the whole century. Yet, so dominant was the 'remnant' approach that even the religious assumed its accuracy.

The very language of the tired clichés ('dwindling congregations', 'darken the doors', 'boring', 'stuffy', 'pompous', 'dogmatic', 'prelate') indicated that religious 'news' came in ritual and mythological forms. It was 'once upon a time' time (smile or snigger to taste). Even the approbation was stereotyped: 'historical' became a synonym for 'old' and 'historic' for 'first' (regardless of its significance, religious or secular), while modernity bred puns about clergy 'revving up' and so on, *ad nauseam*.

Religion is, indeed, inevitably ludicrous because claims to infinity always slip on the banana-skins of finitude, but the laughter has become more aggressive (or defensive) than kind. The brilliant mid-century cartoonist, Giles, made an art-form out of the old, domesticated, parochial stereotypes but the feeling of fond familiarity disappeared with his demise in the 1960s and was replaced by a harsher culture in the 1980s.

Despite long-standing awareness of the eccentricity of the British media, I too was caught out by such widespread American interest in the General Synod vote to ordain women. (I venture to be personal on the grounds that it is real evidence, cited in the belief that it is in some degree representative.) The interest in the Church (and in the Crown) was tinged with fascination at the sight of anachronisms updating themselves, but there was some respect for a reality whose very strangeness called for consideration. This underlying interest has been vastly underestimated, not least in the media and the Churches and by those who pride themselves upon being in touch with what is contemporary and of the 'real' world.

No doubt the Church of England used, of all institutions, to epitomize self-deprecation. Its members could afford to: it was financially secure in the Church Commissioners' endowments, politically confident in its constitutional position and culturally

11

confident in its educational Establishment. In fairness, it was, and it remains, anxious to distance itself from its own tendency to pomposity, both apparent and real. However, it still epitomizes a widespread tendency, at least in the West (and not least among religious leaders), to underestimate the significance of religion in every way.

The third feature of the reaction to that piece of news united the public domain with (dare one say?) the empirical: the 'never-never land' comes down to earth, fantasy is grounded, myth is confronted by reality – but does not even know that it is. 'When ignorance is bliss, 'tis folly to be wise', so journalists stick to their 'fundamentalist' stereotypes of religion, instead of questioning their applicability. For, time and again in the following months and years, the media described the Church of England as 'split from top to bottom' (another standard cliché) over the issue of ordaining women. But it was seven months before a single parishioner so much as mentioned the matter to me. Then, as it happens, it was a 'parishioner' in the traditional Anglican sense: an elderly man who never came to church (except for funerals). He was genuinely puzzled '*why* some of these people [looking at the television screen] don't want women priests' because he simply couldn't understand their reasoning.

A 'great gulf [is] fixed' between public images, which may be doctored with all the artificiality of Marie Antoinette's *toilette*, and private perceptions, which are based upon subjectivities that may be more private than a more ordinary toilet. To some extent the difference is one of age (and could be linked with the tendency of many – not all – congregations to attract those who are older chronologically and/or culturally or spiritually). For, in some instances, the worldview of the media is gradually supplanted by personally formed conclusions that are based upon direct experience. Meanwhile, the 'clanging cymbals' of the public culture make inaudible the wisdom of the simple, the 'quiet in the land'.

The fourth feature of the 1992 vote, which was briefly noted by various observers at the time, was the spirit in which the debate and the subsequent voting 'division' were conducted. Those who disagreed, it was said, really listened to and seemed to have actually heard each other. (Mrs Thatcher, when Prime Minister, was reported as commenting with similar admiration upon a General Synod debate on nuclear disarmament; despite, let it be said, its adopting a different stance to her own.) This feature is paradigmatic, but of future possibilities (to be touched on in the last chapter) rather than of historical background, so it will not be elaborated at this point.

One of the primary 'issues in religion', then, is to avoid sheer misunderstandings, through giving different meanings to similar words through stereotyped 'interpretations' of (projections onto) other people's behaviour and through underestimates of its significance. Conversely, one of the primary issues in religion is to give due recognition to both its large-scale and local actuality. A primary concern is to see religion as it really is: the *general* meaning of 'in three dimensions' in the volume's subtitle.

An appropriate place to begin is with some of the problems experienced by each of three groups that have already been alluded to in turn. This is, in fact, a methodological meaning of the subtitle's 'three dimensions'.

First are 'practitioners' of religion. They include that large proportion of the general public who, even after a generation of being told by members of the other two groups that they are not religious, still believe themselves to be so: who say they 'don't go to church often, but still have [their] own religion [*or* faith]'.

They have been described as 'believing without belonging' (Davie, 1990). However, they might better be described as 'belonging without believing' (Bailey, 1990b) and are almost unanimous in two beliefs – that 'it doesn't matter what you believe' and that 'you don't have to go to Church to be a Christian'. For the English (and perhaps the Scots and the Welsh) are a 'nation of behavers' (Marty, 1975). Thus, the charter myth for their religious behaviour (which is ethical not liturgical in form) is not 'Do this in remembrance of me', but 'Love your neighbour as yourself'.

Second are 'leaders' of religion, defined as those who are willing to take responsibility in and for religion. It includes, therefore, all those holding office, whether by election or by selection, and all those who identify themselves with religion (as 'I' or 'we'): those to whom colleagues at work say, 'You go to church – can you tell me why the Church ...?' By dint of simply participating in the life of the Churches ('organized religion'), in effect they become what the canonically Religious would term a 'Third Order'.

Third are 'students' of religion. Typically, they are scholars from the social, religious and theological sciences and those who 'sit at their feet' but they likewise extend to less focused or dedicated

13

commentators, such as professional journalists or those parochial *voyeurs* of Church life, who say they 'like to read the parish magazine, to see what's going on'.

The ideal-types are clear and are epitomized in Christian terms as, firstly, churchgoers (but including all who 'call themselves Christians'), secondly, clergy and other office-holders and, thirdly, students (of various kinds) of Religion. However, it is equally true that each category largely overlaps with at least one of the others (clergy with churchgoers and/or students, for instance), and (in a Christianly 'perfect' world) each would no doubt overlap with both of the others. Nevertheless, those who occupy more than one role can fairly easily distinguish between their different roles – not always to their personal comfort.

The issues of secular faith are conceptually real, then, because firstly existential, not least for the practitioners of religion – without whom both leadership and study would be confined to the museum and library.

1. For practitioners of religion: explicating the implicit

The last third of the twentieth century was marked by an increasing recognition of the reality of what is implicit. At the end of the 1960s Western correspondents suddenly (it seemed) began to talk of the importance of 'losing [or saving] face', in Southeast and Eastern Asia. No doubt this influenced (if it did not reflect) similar understanding on the part of Western politicians and officials. (They were presumably on the way to becoming 'diplomats' and 'diplomatic' again.) By the 1990s it was acknowledged that both sides in ordinary Western industrial disputes also wanted to be seen to 'walk away with something'. Such 'personal investments' were no longer seen as peculiar to 'foreign' ways of life. Everyone has (or should have) a certain *amour-propre*, which, indeed, goes beyond either tangible results or even public standing.

Not only are such obscure realities recognized as present and important: increasingly there is explicit reference to the 'implicit'. Even when that particular term is not used, the same kind of phenomenon is being referred to in talk of 'subliminal messages' and 'hidden agendas', 'sub-texts' and 'underlying philosophy' and (unconscious) 'mind-set', 'worldview', 'culture', 'attitude' or spirituality.

14

My own interest during the same period in 'implicit religion' has no doubt tended to alert me to this apparent trend (as book-lovers notice bookshops and beer-lovers public houses). Contemporaneously, however, the concept of 'post-modernism' has arisen to describe (and has appealed to) a growing self-awareness – and the growing awareness of such self-awareness.

So much in the whole of this last century has been heading in the same direction. It would be glib to say that Freud caused this interest in all that is hidden from consciousness but he certainly became a symbol of the trend. Perhaps his real contribution lay in his invention of an apparently impersonal vocabulary, such as the subconscious or the *id* (even when in fact it drew upon mythological figures, such as Oedipus or the tribal father), as a way of discussing what was most deeply personal. Just as the ritualization of emotion became marginal, psychology provided a vocabulary that accorded approximately with the prevailing canons of rationality and allowed that which was most intimate, and so became most interesting to each individual (their own subjectivity), to be shared, at least verbally.

Yet the movement of which Freud became the symbol was itself only a part of the whole contemporaneous reaction to its opposite: the increasing prevalence and valuation of 'hard facts'. This movement has given religious practitioners a 'hard time'. (Chapter 2 will look at some of their reactions to that situation.) The implications of some of the expressions associated with religion ('ideology', 'motivation', 'function', 'traditional', 'myth', 'legitimate', 'sanctify') were unclear, whether 'accidentally or on purpose'. They could have been used either neutrally or else to point to mistakes that were either morally innocent or deliberate deceits. (The ambiguities were neatly exploited by editors and publishers, as in the *Observer*'s (1963) headline 'Our image of God must go', with reference to John Robinson's *Honest to God*, or the SCM Press's (1977) *The Myth of God Incarnate*.) So religious practitioners were criticized both for talking inherent non-sense (because it was empirically unverifiable) and for not living up to their profession – and for misleading themselves and/or others, knowingly or not.

To some extent, this is the particular kind of 'hard time' that is to be expected in this environment. For the choice is not between rival emperors, with slightly (if crucially) different christological interpretations, as credal battle standards ('symbols') for rallying round, or between rival kings, with slightly (if crucially) different soteriological and sacramental theologies, whose particular 'rule of life' (*religio*) ran alike for personal faith and for public order (*cuius regio, eius religio*). The difference between such classical or Reformation 'hard times' and current ones may be relative rather than absolute but the choice in contemporary society is cultural rather than communal, psychological rather than political. It is between the publicly (which is not the same as the generally) accepted and the apparently (which is not the same as the empirically) 'eccentric'.

Religious practitioners tend not to do themselves justice in this situation. On the one hand, they too readily accept the challenge and try to respond to it in the terms in which it is presented instead of totally 'turning the tables' on their critics. For instance, if their religion is accused of failing to live up to its ideals, they try to prove that it does live up to them. Or, if they are condemned on account of their (inevitable) personal bias, they modestly fail to return the challenge.

On the other hand, they fail to draw upon the full extent of the riches of even that part of their tradition with which they themselves are familiar. It is hardly news to be told of one's own faults or of one's religious community's failings, when it is *de rigueur* for every act of worship or prayer to include the confession of precisely such inadequacies. Similarly, the doctrine of original sin already expresses the widespread awareness that, while we are inevitably judges in our own cases, our judgement is acknowledged to be as open to question as that of any other seeker after truth. And, while some of these particular terms, such as sin and judgement, are especially prominent in the Christian tradition, the experiences and attitudes which they describe would seem to be present in every religious tradition, if not in every human tradition.

Yet the religious practitioners' failure to do justice to themselves (or, rather, to their faith) may not matter very much, it may be suggested. If they were able to pre-empt every argument, there might be less progress, either in their dialogue or in their own tradition. Further, almost by historical definition, that which is seen as religious is that which has hegemony within any cultural tradition. So, even when opposition to 'religion' seems to have hegemony, it can still be seen as something of a temporary 'blip' (a 'kicking against the pricks') – albeit at a cost of millions of lives. For religious traditions are so highly developed, sophisticated and flexible and so powerful, holistic and pervasive that it is difficult for any substantial deviance from them to achieve real independence, let alone establish absolute autonomy, in the long term.

More significantly, in private, religionists themselves often stress not only the difficulty but even the futility of winning such arguments. Perhaps, however, they should do this more publicly. For in doing so they begin to ask questions about the questions, critique the criticisms, demonstrate the character of the phenomenon under discussion, establish its identity and thus provide living empirical data for joint consideration. So they may show that winning such arguments is not what religion is primarily about. From this point of view, it is rather about all the players enjoying a depth of community that enables them together to level the field and agree the rules of play.

Where religious practitioners may 'let themselves down' is that they may not explain what they are about, even if they demonstrate it in practice. Although they may 'know' it in their heart and live it, they may not 'know' it in their mind and say it. So they may try to answer any and every question because it has been asked, feeling they should be able to do so and, therefore, should try to do so. They may then grasp partial answers, for instance to the question of unmerited suffering (for example, that it can sometimes be redemptive), in the hope that they may seem to be total. Or, inspired by the illumination they have received through part of their tradition, such as a scripture or a rite, a teacher or a community, a goal or a method, they may turn that part into a perfect panacea (and downgrade the rest of their own tradition, let alone all other traditions).

A common thread running through many of the problems experienced by many believers in the religions, then, is the perennial difficulty in describing one's faith, which is inevitably ineffable. Today the problem takes the epistemological form of relating reason and commitment, cause and effect, motive and consequence, intention and function, goal and gift, word and deed.

The ambiguity of a characteristically twentieth-century term, 'rationalization', is symptomatic. It has come to mean finding (with whatever degree of deliberateness) reasons to justify positions already espoused (as a counterbalance to the 'modernist' view of truths as logical deductions from identifiable data). It almost escapes

17

notice that 'giving a reason for the faith that is within you' could involve first the straightforward confession that the faith is indeed a *datum* (given) and second that a search is being openly conducted for reasons why it may be consonant with the rest of reality and, hence, not only comprehensible but viable.

Some of the possible partial responses to the problem of suffering illustrate the point that is made particularly clear by the poverty of English compared with Latin: was the man born blind (in order) 'that' or (with the result) 'that' God may be glorified (John 9: 2–3)? 'That' (*ut*) in the Latin would be clearly specified as introducing a 'final' ('purposive') or a consecutive clause by the concluding verb. The ambiguity of the English, with regard to the degree of (self-) consciousness, is an unfortunate anachronism. It hampers the whole hermeneutic process, ham-stringing both apologetics and analysis. Phenomenology might provide the cure but not if it, too, becomes functional and morphological, omitting the subjective from its objectivity.

The difficulty in making explicit the implicit affects more than simply the rational, intellectual and verbal, however. It affects the corporate life of religious communities and so is a problem for their leaders. It also affects scholars' attempts at understanding religion itself. For it is part of the nature of faith. So it feeds back into the life and thought of religious practitioners and leaders as none of their lives are contained in watertight compartments.

2. For leaders of religion: valuing the occasional

'The people', said F. B. Welbourn (1965) regarding Uganda but no doubt with a wider reference in mind, 'are never so political as the political leaders want them to be, or so religious as the religious leaders think they should be.' To which we might add that they are not so keen on learning as educationists think they ought to be or even so keen on consuming as manufacturers would like them to be. In other words, for whatever reason, society's specialists are always wedded to their own function, while the rest of the population remains relatively holistic and undifferentiated (which, Welbourn implies, is perhaps just as well).

The 'leaders' of religion are necessarily fewer in number than the 'practitioners' but they are just as 'motley a crew'. Indeed, they are even more 'motley', and inevitably so, for in being differentiated from their people they are also differentially differentiated from each other. This is the realm of religion, response, understanding, identity, character, spirit, effervescence, freedom and variety, not of quasi-universal, rational, uniform, monistic reduction. Even families may be planned (e.g. to fit into four-seater cars) but religion must be the last place in which to expect to find uniformity. And the number of religious leaders is, still, legion, for everyone who bears any office or confesses any credence in any of the religions, old or new, is increasingly seen as doing so 'vicariously', on behalf of those who, though inert, are yet 'supporters', in the sense of 'believing in' the religion concerned. They 'belong' to it and it 'belongs' to them, they say (or feel).

The leaders' problem is not, primarily, the relation between the explicit and the implicit, as it is with the 'practitioners'. The leaders may have received training in explaining the faith; they are certainly practised in it. Indeed, they may have so concentrated upon the explication of their religion, that they tend to ignore, or explain away, all that is of faith but is not part of (their particular expression of) their faith tradition.

One example of this tendency was to be seen in the reaction by some religious leaders and practitioners in Britain when the Prince of Wales said that he would prefer to see the Sovereign as 'Defender' of 'Faith' rather than of 'the Faith'. Some religionists consider faith of such a 'quantity' or 'quality' (and they hardly distinguish between these two aspects), to be so unreal and unfocused (which, again, is not the same thing) as to be 'indefensible' anyway. For them it lacks, indistinguishably, both substance and value. Indeed, in keeping with an outwardly measurable, simplistic definition of 'the Faith', they seem to have misunderstood him as wanting to be Defender of 'the Faiths' – which might invite a rerun of the Wars of Religion. (Whether Archbishop Cranmer had in mind the Baptised or the Seeking – whether he recognized the issue or indeed intended both possibilities – by his mention in the communion service of 'the mystical body of thy Son, which is the blessed company of all faithful people' might be of particular interest to the Prince, as Patron of the Prayer Book Society.)

In the abstract or the concrete, the general or the particular, they reflect the oft-quoted 'Parson Thwackum' in Henry Fielding's novel *Tom Jones*: 'When I say religion, I mean the Christian religion, and when I say the Christian religion, I mean the Protestant religion, and when I say the Protestant religion, I mean the Church of England, as by law Established'. In his defence, it could be said that at least the parson knew where he stood and, by confessing that position, to some degree transcended it. Is it possible for any one, initially, to say more than, 'When I say a human being, I mean myself, and others, insofar as I am thereby able to enter into their existence'? (cp. Bailey, 1997a: 89–90).

The theme running through the various problems felt by those carrying responsibility in religion could be described as 'visibility' rather than explication. The problem may be similar but the medium of its expression is different. The leaders' position could be summed up as: 'I know the people say they believe; all right, I suppose they do sincerely mean it, at least when they're saying it; and yes, I know they're nice to their neighbours (others things being equal); but religion is deeper and broader than prudence or manners, and what have they to show on that account? What difference does their faith make in their lives? How does it affect the way they actually spend their time, talents and money or what they say or feel about things? How much does their belief cost them? Are their chips ever down?'

The problem for the leader is the relationship not between his own believing and speaking, as for the practitioners, but between their believing and their doing or his belief and their (in)action. The problem lies in the sphere of visible, not verbal, expression. Indeed, leaders may pay very careful attention to their own or others' verbalizing of the faith, in preaching, worship or catechetical teaching for instance, but can become quite careless of others' statements of faith. They may seek to cover their boredom with popular forms of expression ('I believe in Christianity', for instance) by dismissing them as platitudinous or suspecting their sincerity (Bailey, 1997a: 259–62).

We may find it difficult to understand why those who regularly confess their own faith should find others' untutored use of the only forms available to them to be of less significance, or to understand how any witness of the speaker's body language, hesitation or intonation could possibly doubt the significance of such a confession of faith for the one confessing it. A teacher, for instance of religious education, who has heard it all so often before, would not accede to boredom with or suspicion of any such 'first steps'. This 'care-less-ness' may also, therefore, camouflage the embarrassment felt when those who have grown accustomed to confessing their own faith in a polished ritual form meet with a parallel that is more spontaneous or homespun.

Whatever the reason, be it a flight from the personal or zeal for the cause, the leaders of religion can become painstaking accountants of such items as the attendance at services and upkeep of buildings, which they (perhaps above all) say does not count ultimately and so (they sometimes also say) cannot ultimately be counted significant at all. The paradox has long occasioned comment as in the medieval conundrum, 'whether an archdeacon *can* be saved' or the test of preaching sometimes found among Lutherans, as the *absence* of hearers, or the 1960s suggestion that secularization was the virtual coming of the Kingdom.

The problem is part of the interface between the sacred and the secular, which is inevitably ludicrous (like finding the mid-point between one and infinity). It is, however, a peculiarly Judeo-Christian or even Western problem (*Oriental Studies*, 1987). Should such systemic contrasts develop in the less uniformitarian religions of India and China, say, they might occur as a result of a concern for the cultural heritage or for bureaucratic statistics and so seem less fundamentally or religiously contradictory or paradoxical.

The problem faced by the leader is epitomized in the change of meaning undergone by 'occasional'. It impacts directly and practically upon the life of the Church of England, for instance, through the description of baptism and confirmation, ordination and the visitation of the sick and the marriage and funeral services as 'occasional offices' (regardless of the question of their sacramental status). Indeed, the loss of the earlier significance of 'occasion-al', not only arose from the reduced sense of community and continuity in society and religion, but also seemed to legitimate a low-level interpretation by the clergy of the motives of those seeking the more popular of these rites.

When 'occasional' inferred the sense of (an) occasion, which demonstrated, by its happening, the significance of the event and its commemoration, both in the passage of time and in the lives of those participating, then the ceremony was a 'mark' (or marque) to be borne and be judged by, a temporal marker which marked one forever. But when 'occasional' was seen as meaning not so much 'significant' as 'spasmodic', not so much 'indelible' as 'odd', not so much 'permanent' as 'past', not so much 'rare' as 'casual', not so much 'one-off' as 'optional', not so much 'special' as 'whimsical', then the motivation behind requests for the more popular of the occasional offices was dismissed as social, at best, or at worst as magical, superstitious or hypocritical.

Those for whom specifically religious activities are part of weekly or even daily life can overlook the personal significance (religious as well as social) which occasional participation can hold for others. Just as it takes more effort to adjust one's schedule in order to participate at all, so the memory of the experience may linger on for years. The same is true, of course, of other non-repeating events: graduation photographs jostle with wedding photos in most family dwellings now. They testify to not just a past day but a continuing status. The photograph bears witness to a moment that was momentous, albeit momentary. It has momentum.

Leaders of religion, like 'elders' in other aspects of human life, must encounter some problem or other in the course of which to exercise their vocation. Time was, in western Europe for instance, when the issues might have been theological or political. The relation of the part to the whole took the form not of the relationship of the occasional to the continuous but of the relationship of the spiritual to the material (and the relationship of the matter of the sacrament to ordinary matter). If the issues now largely revolve around time and humanity and hence meaning, they can be seen as consonant with much else that is currently observable in human life as is demonstrated, indeed, by this very way of contextualizing such problems – in terms of changes in consciousness.

Now, though, the significance of the temporal dimension has outstripped that of the spatial dimension in religion as in experience generally (Panikkar, 1978). Distance is increasingly measured in hours and as clocks were successively given minute hands and watches second hands, so the present has become more existentially real and the past apparently less meaning-full.

3. For students of religion: gauging the transcendent

Practitioners of religion, inevitably unable adequately to articulate their faith, may begin to doubt its distinctive reality through becoming entangled in reductionist nets. Leaders of religion, looking for the works in which religious faith is expected to issue, may tend to write off other forms of faith as unreal and/or unworthy. For students of religion, however, the problem is to measure the transcendent element within faith.

The notion of infinity provides a useful metaphor for the element of transcendence within faith. The religious practitioner (not surprisingly) has difficulty in describing his/her experience of that 'infinity', without belittling it. A very large number, however large, is not even half way to it. It is scarcely nearer to *infinity* than a very small number. Indeed, 'infinity' can, as we say, be infinitely small as well as infinitely large.

If the analogy disappoints, then that disappointment can be both 'humbling' ('of the humus', the *fertile* topsoil) and productive. For leaders, accustomed to the management of sites and contexts for our apprehending of infinity and our apprehending by Infinity, may find difficulty in apprehending such apprehensions as occur elsewhere and lead to different results. But the secular student is ultimately trying to give such 'infinity' a value, if only in terms of its gravitational pull. A successful search for its power will raise questions as to whether the observer's 'finite' interpretation necessitates the actor's sense of infinity. An unsuccessful search for an empirical consequence of infinity should prompt questions as to whether its invisibility is either due to its non-existence or to its ubiquity (the fish-in-the-water syndrome).

The modern study of religion has many forebears. Gautama Siddhartha, for instance, sat at the feet of many religious teachers before evolving his own, 'Middle', Way. His search for the Truth was deliberate and painstaking, conscious and conscientious (in ordinary speech, both religious and scientific). Such resulting tra[ns]ditions are meant to be transferred and handed on. Some, indeed, are committed to writing 'for our learning'. The fact that their originators saw themselves as talking either about life (Bouquet, 1954) or else about God does not prevent us (it seems) from describing their teachings, and hence their students' concern, as being a third thing altogether: 'religious'. However, the secular study of religion impoverishes itself unnecessarily if it regards such traditions simply as objects for study and we ignore the results of millennia of reflection upon results, combining theory and experiment, analysis and application.

Nevertheless, Religious Studies, as an academic rather than a

23

spiritual discipline, is relatively novel. In the first place, it is ostensibly not intended to be itself a religious quest. It may help us to understand people but is not specifically intended to help us in understanding life. In the second place it is, ideally, magpie-like, totally non-discriminatory. Third, whereas magic assumes that the object of its endeavour is manipulable and science assumes that, though passive, it has substance, Religious Studies tends to assume that its core (the sacred) has consequences and may have characteristics of its own. However, it is assumed to be without any will of its own.

Buddhism may have had to wait before being included within the subject matter of the discipline. However, the Buddha's apparent personal reluctance even to ask, let alone answer, questions regarding his own beliefs about divinity is thoroughly consonant with Religious Studies' own approach. That this should have hindered, rather than helped, the inclusion of his tradition is symptomatic both of a determined natural–supernatural dualism and of the conviction that a new Enlightenment had occurred. This reticence could be described as a necessary antidote to the overly personalized divinity of much of Protestantism and the overly dichotomized supernaturalism of much of Catholicism. Judaism's reluctance to name the Infinite is consonant with it; it deals with the problems of the interface between the finite and the infinite in narrative form. Islam's stark, existential juxtaposition of Allah's will and compassion offers an alternative solution to the problem of combining the positive and the negative aspects of faith.

If the ultimate core of religious studies be compared, then, with the 'God' of the Hebrew scriptures, we have a model for the final object of the discipline being highly personal: idiosyncratic, emotional, self-willed, indescribable, yet responsive (Exodus 3: 14). Lacking material form or peer group, however, 'he' is unclassifiable and uniquely unique. The point is delightfully illustrated by the apophatic traditions' use of the most appropriate and accustomed comparisons (Father, loving, present, eternity, existence, etc.) only in order immediately to deny them.

Thus, being 'personal' (if 'he' can be tentatively described in any way; *vide* Chapter 4), this 'object' (which is pure subject) can be addressed by his 'personal' Name (and can promise to hear), yet cannot be located (e.g. as a member of a class). Reverence, such as we sometimes find echoes of when discussing the dead, dictates that,

24

when speaking about him rather than to him, a periphrasis be used (as in Islam) or, of course, silence maintained (as in early Buddhism and in Religious Studies).

Thus the belief itself follows the object of that belief in being *sui generis* and, therefore, simultaneously and inevitably unprovable except through the witness of 'religion' and of life itself. For his, and our, silence is otherwise ambiguous. It could be a mark of respect for his ubiquitous presence or the consequence of his unreality. It could signify reverence or denial.

In terms of Religious Studies, the problem becomes one of validating transcendence. This tends to become operationalized in exercises designed to see whether the distinctively religious has measurable and therefore traceable causes or consequences (Hay, 1982). This assumes, however, that the experience of transcendence is restricted to the exceptional. If it can be classified as 'natural' because usual, then it is not after all transcendent, according to this understanding of transcendence, religion and life (Oman, 1931; Bailey, 2000).

If spelt out, such a 'theology' would leave most religious practitioners (of whatever ilk) dumbstruck. They thought their belief was primarily to do with the ordinary, the usual. That is what popular religion (and superstition and magic) have always been about: to make use of the incomprehensible was natural, rather than supernatural. (The reversion of 'supernatural', since about 1970, to this non-dichotomous meaning is part of the change from modernity to post-modernity discussed in Chapter 4.)

Extraordinary attention to the extra-ordinary tends to be suspect, to the mind of regular practitioners, as intellectually superstitious, psychologically obsessive, spiritually immature, practically magical and theologically idolatrous. Thus the Alister Hardy Centre for Research into Religious Experience has found a third of the population (or even two-thirds) believe themselves to have had a religious experience (which, usually, they have never previously shared with anyone) but Sir Alister himself had to repeatedly invite regular religious practitioners, not least from the mainstream Churches, to submit any reports at all.

The student of religion is in a cleft stick. If (s)he assumes that religion is unique, not only in the way that every phenomenon is unique but in a uniquely unique way (*sui generis*), then, in so far as (s)he focuses on the specifically religious dimensions of such

25

experience, there is nothing useful to say because whatever is said cannot 'make sense'. The phenomenon may be absolute, like Allah, but it is simply itself: it is its own, isolated sense (cp. the Greek *idios*, private). If, on the other hand, the student demonstrates the consonance even of the religious, with everything else that 'makes sense' in the context, (s)he runs a twofold danger: either the religious or the secular becomes the merely automated consequence of the other. One of them loses its autonomy.

The peculiar character of moral 'compulsion' aids and abets the confusion, for conscience says, 'I can [*sic*] no other'. Phenomenologically, the problem lies in the meeting of two wills (comparable to an irresistible force meeting an immovable object). Linguistically, it is epitomized in the confusion of 'will' with 'shall' (in the popular understanding of the marriage vows, for instance), and 'shall' with 'will' (in weather forecasts, for instance). Here, the Latin did not help: the 'future simple' tense (*amabo*, I will/shall love) failed to distinguish between a statement of purpose and a prediction. It is a perennial problem: to say what one anticipates a group that one is involved in will decide tends to be taken as a statement of preference. The ambiguity of 'expect' is paradigmatic, as in Nelson's famous signal: 'England expects that every man will do his duty'.

Concern for the value of such a truth as is indicated in '*can* do no other' and respect for colleagues may transmute the ambiguous and catastrophic 'you must' into 'we should'. But it also prompts the opposite reaction, 'You are deceived: it is only you who "can" do other'. The sense of moral compulsion, starting as a 'divine inspiration' but sliding into ethical imperialism, inspires an equal and opposite moral reaction, which slides into moral negativism. If conscience itself is 'deified', then the opposing conscience is 'atheised' and moral 'compulsion' becomes mechanistic 'causation'. If freedom is threatened by belief, free will is denied by disbelief, or so believers believe. If divine revelation is claimed in self-justification, then all revelation is denied in self-defence.

The position of Religious Studies is not dissimilar. A *sui generis* religiosity may be seen either as dominant or as irrelevant. An epiphenomenal religion may be seen either as subservient or as insignificant. The need is for a model of religion which allows the phenomenon itself sufficient reality to interact with the secular, neither as dictator nor as toady but in the unrelaxed, creative partnership of a dialectical dialogue.

Postlude: the disciples' dilemma

The problem involved in the issue of religion for practitioners of it may be illustrated by an incident recounted by a Christian minister, who probably spoke, unconsciously, for people of all faiths and all people of faith.

I had asked the members of a group starting an adult education class in 'implicit religion' to share with the rest of us some incident (or some artefact, any human 'product') which had shown them what a person (or some group of people) stood for. It was the kind of question people ask when someone dies, as they contemplate what they have received and have now lost, which might become the theme of a memorial service, which recognizes the need for a combination of thanksgiving and condolence. When reporting back, following discussion in pairs, it transpired that the members had found the question difficult. They could not tune into the memory, at the drop of a hat, of any moment that had revealed some body's (a plural or individual body's) commitment(s), what they believed in, what gave coherence to their life and 'brought them to life', their particular 'genius', the 'soul' that was unique (and thus also 'sole').

Eventually this particular member of the group proffered:

> I don't know whether this is the sort of thing you are looking for, but I would *like* to tell you about something that happened to me last night.

> I had to take my dogs to be vaccinated, and I couldn't use my car, so another priest gave me a lift. There was a *locum* on duty, instead of the usual vet. When he realized I was a minister, he said he'd been to a Pet Service the previous evening at — Church, in aid of the RSPCA. 'It was terrific,' he said. 'After all, that's what Christianity's all about, isn't it?'

> 'What absolute rubbish,' said my colleague, when I told him about this conversation on the way home. 'It's got nothing to do with Christianity.'

> It's left me feeling quite uncomfortable.

The answer to his opening comment was that the story was not quite what I was anticipating: I was hoping for stories that revealed people's ordinary non-ecclesiastical commitments, if only in order to direct attention away from what is usually seen as religion and on to life as a whole. I was wanting to show how 'secular' life might receive additional illumination (additional to all the other ways in which we regard it, from the perspectives of economics, politics,

27

history, psychology, and so on), if we also regard it as sometimes putatively containing within itself something like its own religion. However, as it happens the minister had produced a rather 'religious' story, in the accustomed sense. Yet it served the purpose of revealing an 'implicit religion', even though in this case it took some 'ordinary' religious forms. Indeed, his account revealed three different implicit religions, and whether they were expressed in or fitted in with traditional Christian shapes was hard to say and (from our then point of view) was not the question.

The vet volunteered his revelation of his own implicit religion (encouraged by the sight of his client's clerical collar and his conviction that the service had been so 'Christian'). Perhaps he had responded to this recognition by the Church of that combination of idealism and patience, skill and dedication that went to make up his 'vocation'. Clearly he had not dismissed the event, before or afterwards, as merely giving *carte blanche* for sentimentality, a gimmicky device to fill the church at any cost or as simple performance. His desire to share his 'good news' was inspired by delight, although he might also have seen it as an invitation for the minister to 'go and do likewise' and arrange similar services.

The apparent speed, clarity and vehemence of the priest's reaction might arise from 'faith speaking to faith': it immediately recognized its polar opposite, at another point on the same continuum. The priest obviously knew the 'epiphany' of Divinity in Christ and a continuing 'hierophany' in bread and wine and, perhaps, in the world. So, when the vet found a hierophany in the Church's becoming 'worldly', he became, for the priest, not merely an unbeliever but a heretic and, therefore, a dangerous menace. The believer may merely 'pass by on the other side' of unbelief or disbelief but recognizes mis-belief at once.

The raconteur may be described as the minister, a middle-man. He says little about himself, except that he wants to tell us about the two conversations, and that they have left him feeling 'uncomfortable'. It is clear, however, that each man felt free with him to express (or confess) their own faith and that he has 'stored' both and so is still listening 'that he might understand'. Doubly challenged, he is buffeted but not 'blown about'. Simultaneously stretched in opposing directions, he yet retains his own identity, standing upright still.

Or, as the chief executive of a sizeable organization reported that he used to say to managers who confessed to having problems: 'Good, otherwise you'd have no job'. The practitioner, leader and student of religion all 'have a job': to understand people and therefore to regard them holistically but, as no one is called to attempt everything, in particular to understand them from the particular perspective of whatever goes to make up their *intentionality*.

2. Reactions

Prelude: 'modernizing' Methodism

At its annual conference in June 1999 the Methodist Church in Great Britain discussed whether 'exploring' rather than 'believing' could be a sufficient basis for membership. They also discussed their Church's declining membership; whether alcohol might be allowed on church premises; and whether advantage might be taken of grants from the National Lottery. The presenter of BBC Radio 4's 'Sunday' programme of religious news, expressing sympathy with the conference for having to debate four such issues at one conference, interviewed two of the participants, who described all the issues in terms of 'moving with the times' and 'involving the relationship of the sacred and the secular'.

It was indicated in the previous chapter that the explicit is less important than the implicit from the point of view of understanding either religious behaviour in particular or human behaviour in general. Indeed, the explicit could be seen as a means to the end of understanding the implicit: communication as a valuable means to the end of achieving communion, as the outward and visible symbol of an inward and (otherwise) invisible truth. Nevertheless, words and ideas, concepts and analyses do matter, so long as people strive to take corporate decisions cooperatively. Leadership without shared reasoning is dictatorship; democracy without argument would be government without consent. Actual confusion, or mere lack of clarity, can lead to emotional frustration and loss of practical faith or hope. Prayer, without full understanding, is normal, but prayer *contrary* to *all* understanding must remain rare.

It is important, therefore, to think and speak as clearly as we are able in this most passionate but least effable of areas. For instance, the first of the expressions from the interviews just quoted ('moving

31

with the times') could be understood, at least as it stands, as equating historical process with religious progress, turning the *Zeitgeist* into the Holy Ghost and confusing fatalism with Providence; while the second, 'the relationship of the sacred with the secular', appears to oppose 'sacred' (which involves subjectivity) to 'secular' (which Chapters 3 and 4 suggest is a sociological if not a legal concept), and yet seems to treat them as categorially 'equal and opposite' to each other.

The difficulties of analysis are considerable. (They will be illustrated in Chapter 3.) Effort is required if we are to 'fix' the 'moment' of a religious experience or argument, to suspend judgement (even of intention), to envisage the whole range of possible interpretations and finally to consider those hypotheses that remain viable. Such minute 'atoms' of experience, however, share with their physical counterpart not only their complexity and near-invisibility but also both their ability to reveal the structure of so much beyond themselves and above all the power that their 'explosion' generates.

So a deliberate pursuit of wisdom in religious practise, leadership and study is necessary, if only to drive out folly. Otherwise we find ourselves running round the rat-race described by the anthropologist G. C. Baëta at another Methodist conference, this time in West Africa in 1965:

> Whatever others may do in their own countries, our people *live* with their dead ... . Yet when Church bodies make rulings on the matter of funeral observance, the reasons given for the repressive measures ... are not even religious reasons, but merely such irrelevancies as expense, inconvenience, and waste of time. So the decisions get nowhere, and the problems persist.
>
> (Sundkler, 1962: ch. V, quoted in Bailey, 1997a: 28)

In this passage, Baëta tries to jolt the 'Church bodies' into realizing the real significance of 'their dead' by neatly adopting the parallel strategy of reducing 'expense', etc. to an 'irrelevancy'. Each side of the argument was, of course, religious for those who held it; to dismiss the opposition as less than religious (at least for its protagonists) was the perfect recipe for talking past one another. Subsequently, no doubt, dialogue developed as each party divined the religious dimension within the other's attitudes: that the 'departed' had gone away physically but continued to be present in spirit and that the desire for economy arose from philanthropic concerns that were equally, albeit differently, spiritual in character.

So this chapter will try to summarize, as themselves religious phenomena, some current religious reactions to some contemporary religious issues.

1. Denying identity: conformity, insincerity and apathy

As historical studies and statistical surveys of North America, Britain and even of the Early Church multiply, it seems apparent that the overt religious practitioner has often been in a minority. In England churchgoers were at least relatively numerous in the Victorian period and, perhaps, between the mid-sixteenth and mid-seventeenth centuries. However, even for those periods we cannot assume that churchgoers composed a majority of the population or that churchgoing was popular (in either sense). Even when churchgoers were relatively numerous, moreover, it is not unreasonable to suppose (judging by Pepys's Diaries, for instance) that the 'genuinely religious' ones were still in a relative minority.

Questioning the myth that 'in the old days everyone went to church' raises the further question of the myth's origins. As the myth used to hang over current religionists (and others) somewhat like a mushroom cloud, always suggesting depressing comparisons, the issue is of more than academic importance. 'Ethnomethodological'-type reasons may be suggested: the Sundays when people went to church stood out in the memory, if only because they were different, and the relative popularity of certain occasions meant that those who only went then never saw inside the church on other, 'ordinary' Sundays. Psychologically and anthropologically, however, there is also a recurrent tendency to place Golden Ages in the past (Wilson, 1971), especially in small-scale societies (of which the family is an example, see Chapter 4), and so to turn the past, including one's own youth, into such a Golden Age.

The problem of numbers, then, is not a new issue. It is not even as great an issue as it was in the nineteenth century when the various denominations, local churches and individuals devoted vast efforts to the provision of buildings. In a score of years, in the 1820s and 1830s, the vicar of Leeds, 'Dean Hook' (so called because he was subsequently Dean of Chichester Cathedral), built a score not only of churches but also of schools and of parsonages. Today, so far as the Churches in Britain are concerned, although the cupboard threatens to be empty in the future, there is recovery of confidence regarding the present, if only because the 'glorious' past has at last almost passed away, out of historical memory.

If the problem of numbers is not the primary issue, because not so novel, neither is that of culture. Certainly there were times, notably in the Middle Ages, when the Church 'enjoyed' (as they say) cultural hegemony or so it tends to seem, if only because organized religion left the best evidence. But usually, if not always, religious practitioners have tended to be so preoccupied with the ways in which their world falls short of the Kingdom (in Christian terminology) that they hardly even notice (let alone render thanks for) the ways in which the Kingdom they seek is itself constantly 'coming' under their very noses but often outside 'church'. So 'the faithful' probably always feel beleaguered. If the issue for them today is whether anyone can or will 'hear', at least they can enjoy considerable, if not complete, freedom of speech.

The issue today is rather one of identity (which may be the modern term for 'soul'). The problem takes several forms. For religious practitioners feel they should 'stand up and be counted' in different ways and in the various contexts in which they find themselves; so they feel guilty about not doing so. Their hesitation tends to be blamed upon simple cowardice but often it could equally be said to arise from uncertainty as to the right method to adopt. This in its turn could have been thought through in advance with other practitioners, leading to a growth in fellowship, as well as in wisdom. It can also be suggested that their reluctance to speak out actually arises from their reading of the spirit of the moment and that their wish to witness, producing within them a silent suffering, may itself be the best witness. However, another reason for their hesitation is sheer uncertainty as to what constitutes the core of Christian identity and whether that core constitutes their own identity.

A recent public example in the United Kingdom was the 'keeping' of the millennium. Britain was among a small group of countries (apparently) that tried to observe the anniversary in various corporate ways. This ability to acknowledge the reality of a religious event was in keeping with the Establishment of the Churches of England and Scotland, arising out of history but reflecting the continuing 'establishment' of a not-very-ecclesiastical form of Christianity. Fearful on the one side of sharing in anything less than a full-blooded exposition of the Gospel and on the other side of offending those of other faiths or none, neither the Churches nor the government could identify a theme (be it the influence of Jesus or engineering) for a common celebration that would have recognized both the reality and differences of conviction. The result was vapid.

Another form taken by the problem of self-identification is a reluctance to identify either with their own religions, as public organizations, or with others who identify themselves by the same label. Churchwardens of different parishes, for instance, can work in adjacent offices for years without discovering that they share their religious practise, role and identity. This must be seen in the whole context of alienation (Baum, 1975) which, if the Hebrew 'right-eousness' indicates 'right *relationships*', could be seen as the modern word for 'un-righteousness'. The relative success of religious institutions, at least when compared with other voluntary organizations, is at last beginning to be appreciated by political practitioners, if not yet by religious ones. But that very 'success' is no doubt reflected in the recurring 'hard times', whether they take the form of conscious or unconscious 'ignor-ance' or of straightforward persecution.

In these circumstances, the individual tends (or is 'tempted') to conform to the social environment and hopes to pass unnoticed. However, this rarely works, for the religious practitioner is usually a marked person, not least for those who do not practise. Any desire for anonymity, respect for others' freedom or willingness to bide one's time too easily leads to the suspicion that the practitioners are neither sincere in their own profession nor truly 'one of us' as they 'pretend'.

The repression of such religious faith and hope, on the part of both practitioners and their observers, leads to anger and thus to apathy: an inability to suffer – in this case the pain of entering into dialogue. For the dialogue that is possible in contemporary society involves as much effort and self-discipline as the individualistic rules-of-life that catechumens were taught from the sixteenth to the nineteenth century and the communal Rules of Life that operated in the medieval monastic Orders. It requires, for instance, patience to listen and effort to understand, courage to confess and effort to explain, and the constant recognition that participants both identify with what they say and yet are not identical with it.

2. Maximizing difference: ritual, dogma and culture

Religious leaders have inevitably tended to respond to their problems by maximizing the differentiation provided by their religion. Christians, for instance, have stressed new life following a conversion experience, the Word of God as found in sacred scripture, the divine origin of Holy Church or the utter uniqueness of the Son of Man. Those who minimized the difference either resigned or were bypassed: seen, at best, as believing in the whole (the Kingdom) rather than in 'their' part of it (the Church). In the nature of things 'new societies' (like the United States) and new religious societies (such as task-oriented voluntary groups) have tended to set a particular pattern because they blazed a trail, suggesting that, to be 'real', religion must be 'different' from ordinary life.

However, older religious bodies, as trail-blazers in their day, have also set a pattern. For instance, they are partly responsible for the very definition of 'religion' (see Chapter 5), which can now increasingly be seen as a 'political' issue (Bromley and Greil, forthcoming). Thus the leaders' tendency to undervalue the significance of the 'occasional', be it a wedding or a veterans' annual ceremony, arose out of their expectation that, if participation in ritual was not both frequent and regular, its meaning must be social not religious, festive not serious, ceremonial not spiritual, nostalgic rather than moral. Religion can be a real dimension of life, despite being neither novel nor frequent.

This tendency to undervaluation takes various forms and operates in various directions. One direction has already been mentioned: a heightened expectation of the ordinary practitioner. Parents wanting their baby to be baptized, for instance, have been expected not only to desire the ceremony and promise to honour its meaning later, but also (often) to undergo instruction in the faith and attend worship first. An element of prior purification (credal and ritual as well as moral) has been insisted upon. Indeed, this issue has sometimes divided denominations and local churches into two groups, hinging upon the demands of the leaders and the meaning of true leadership and of true discipleship.

There are a variety of theological justifications for such policies. Religiously, however, the common motivation hinges upon what is often described as a renewed sense of the holiness of God. That way of describing the inspirational experience, however, is circular. Indeed, its leaders sometimes said, 'Let God be God'. Certainly, this demonstrates its self-authenticating character. However, to avoid truisms that contain their ultimate predicate in their original syndicate, and thus open up the conviction for discussion, it might be rephrased as an insistence upon the differentness of the Divine (cp. Job 38–39 as against even Exodus 3: 14).

The history of the Church of England shows two key moments in this development. Indeed, it is not accidental that their symbolic significance was first realized not by historians but by those involved at the time. Thus they can be dated precisely: 24 May 1709 and 17 July 1833. Significant in the rise of the Evangelical and Oxford Movements respectively, they form a contrasting pair ecclesiastically, yet phenomenologically they are similar and, religiously, parts of a single developmental process.

Both happened in a religious gathering on a Sunday; in each a man called John received or imparted a new experience or vision. On the first occasion, John Wesley felt his 'heart strangely warmed' in a prayer meeting at Aldersgate in London. On the second, John Keble preached his sermon on the Church as a divine institution to the assize judges in the University Church at Oxford (John Henry Newman being among those affected subsequently).

Whatever inter- and intra-denominational loyalties may have made of the two men's philosophies, Religious Studies cannot but see them as respectively inward and outward, 'personal' (meaning subjective) and institutional, examples or expressions of the same type of religious experience or conviction. Indeed, each was an experience not so much of life or of Divinity as of what it meant to be religious. The issue was bound to arise as an intellectual and ethical issue, following the decline of holistic monastic practice and the growing emphasis upon the subjective dimension of personal existence. It was the inner, religious form of the 'experimental' method espoused by the nascent natural sciences.

In their own individual ways and in their own socio-religious contexts, the majority of religious leaders in the various western European countries since the Wars of Religion (Pascal, Schleiermacher, Grundtvig, etc.), have probably followed similar routes. In this context, the influence of the Wesley brothers and the wider Evangelical Revival and of the Oxford Movement and the wider Catholic Revival have transformed the religious life of the Churches (if not of the people) in England and elsewhere almost beyond recognition. So much in Church life, from choirs to synods, seminaries to rules of life, clerical collars to missionary societies, that in the twentieth century was taken as 'normal' and so assumed to be permanent (but is now fast changing) only became general in the middle of the nineteenth century as a consequence of this new understanding of what 'religion' entailed.

The common thread running through all these instances, as has been said, was the need for 'religion' to have an identity of its own because Divinity itself is what is felt to be, and so should be seen to be, different from humanity, as the supernatural was assumed to be different from the natural. Belief in the Incarnation, as revealing their ultimate unity, and in the crucifixion as at-one-ing them again, positively encouraged emphasis upon their prior duality.

Behaviourally it affected 'ritual' activities. The term, which had been liturgical (i.e. to do with *public* 'works', such as civic games), now contracted, becoming purely religious. So its twentieth-century 'borrowing' to describe non-religious behaviour (for example Moore and Myerhoff, 1977), at first seemed metaphorical and light-hearted (or downright provocative). Historical studies of ecclesiastical ritual blossomed as they had not done since the Middle Ages, when (as usual in small-scale societies, with Golden Ages placed in the past) precedent legitimated power. So complete was the change in the meaning of ritual, religion and divinity around the end of the eighteenth century (and then again, in reverse, towards the end of the twentieth century) that it may be doubted whether its emotional or practical significance, though felt at the time by both its proponents and opponents, has yet been fully grasped by religious leaders, participants or observers.

The filling of the church building with pews and the ideological expulsion of 'secular' activities from the church building, for instance, led to the building first of what were called 'church schools' and then of what were called 'church halls'. Vestries were also built for such ancillary and therefore secular needs (albeit accompanied by prayer) as the minister's vesting and divesting of robes and the storage of candles and flower-vases, so that the sanctuary and church might be unsullied by the practicalities of dress and domesticity. As the twentieth century closed, however, the Church of England discarded the Oxford Movement's particular propagation of the holy, by serving coffee in church, and including within the public service the final preparations for it, such as the entry of the Gospel (book) and the lighting of candles (as the Orthodox have never ceased doing).

Turning from the behavioural to the mental, the change involved emphasizing the differentness of Divinity, as has already been said. There is a renewed danger of circularity, however. For, in the context of the written word, the mental aspect of the change can too easily be assumed to be its motor. This was, indeed, a characteristic assumption of the time in question (to which both Marx and Freud, for instance, were reacting). Hence a preference, as the twenty-first century dawns, for 'mental' rather than (say) 'intellectual', for 'Divinity' (albeit with an initial capital) rather than 'God' – and generally for the religious (in this case, religious experience and religiosity) rather than theology and for situating Religious Studies within Social Studies rather than philosophy, as a study of function rather than ontology ('religion is as religion does').

Some of the institutional, symbolic or sacramental ways in which the change in perception was expressed have already been alluded to. Their common existential core was a felt need for conversion. This was seen either as a momentary experience or decision or as a life-long process, or as both. Indeed, the minute investigation of liturgical history was balanced by the nuanced exploration of spiritual development in the light of Pauline, Patristic and Reformation teaching about justification and sanctification. An Episcopalian may find a Methodist lay preacher's familiarity with such concepts nothing less than esoteric, just as a Methodist may find Anglican concern with the 'apostolic succession' (in the consecration of bishops), the English may find Scottish concern for theology, or the British may find American discussion of 'creation-ism' and the various forms of 'millennialism'.

However, it is this sense of differentness that leads most non-experts to see 'theology' as splitting hairs over matters beyond head knowledge, all attempts to teach religion as 'indoctrination', and the confession of what is perceived as inconvenient but unavoidable *data* as the self-indulgence of a wilful 'dogmatism'. Sometimes, indeed, that does appear to be part of their motivation. The Anglo-Catholic layman W. G. Ward (1802–82) said he would like a Papal Bull with

39

his copy of *The Times* each morning. Pride sometimes seems to be taken in believing '*because* it is impossible'. Theology is used in order to put others down. Worship provides opportunity to display ritual prowess. Fellowship is a context for competition.

It was difficult for Christian religious groups in Western societies to establish the third or social aspect of their religious life as distinct in a communal sense. It was also difficult to establish a separate morality. This resulted in the development of a particular culture, in the sense of a *way* of thinking and judging, feeling and relating. Closely related to educability (the *Book of Common Prayer* had sought to be 'edifying' since 1559), and to universities that were founded in the Middle Ages or to schools that began in the sixteenth century, the desire to be different encouraged the burgeoning of new institutions and sometimes seemed inseparable from them. Indeed, in the Church of Scotland in the eighteenth century it was argued that education must precede evangelism for the latter to be worthwhile. Gradually, however, this 'culture' has distinguished itself from education (and education from this culture) and seen its distinctness as lying rather within its particular 'ethos' or, even, 'spirit'.

By the end of the twentieth century, the spiritual (and the Spirit) had come into its own again, at least in theory. If the eighteenth century was the century of a 'Unitarian' Father and the nineteenth and twentieth were the centuries first of the Son of God and then of the Son of Man, the twenty-first century could be that of the spirit and the Spirit, free-floating or focused in the Trinity.

3. Ignoring evidence: categories, experience and humanness

It would be possible to paint a biographical picture of students of religion reacting to their experience. Indeed, there is something highly contrived in any book's blurb about its author, for instance, which describes his/her educational background and academic posts, family situation and research interests but omits all mention of the author's own experience of religion. Direct experience or indirect, positive reaction or negative, how else can one know the very meaning of religion or religious in the text itself? The blurb's value as an aid to understanding authors is demonstrated by the short *Vitae* with which texts are introduced in Jacques Waardenburg (1973) but then he defines 'classical' in part by the authors' death.

For some scholars study is a positive contribution to religion. For others it is an alternative way of participating in something they cannot let go. Even as a conscious process, this need not be condemned morally: having seen the falsity and/or harmfulness of the phenomenon, or of its proponents, they may wish to save their fellows from credulity. As an unconscious process, however, the issue would be spiritual rather than moral. This interpretation would see them as having failed, for whatever reason, to make the successive leaps into self-identification and differentiation. So they seem 'bound' to find reason for any alternative faith that is within them.

Such possibilities need sketching because the scholar is a human being. Shakespeare could have given us a splendid picture of this, along the lines of Henry V's self-portrait of kingship; Dickens, had he been to Oxbridge, might have given us a Reverend Doctor (instead of Mr) Gradgrind. The constant quest for objectivity, impersonality, rationality and universality is admirable, will always be necessary and should remain an ideal. It contains, however, two dangers: the belief that it is possible of achievement and the belief that it, and it alone, is wholly desirable. Now that the mechanical model of the universe has become available to us (metaphorically and experientially), we cannot afford to ignore its practical or conceptual potential (for arranging social benefits, for instance), but we cannot afford to be intoxicated by its potential for organizing 'final solutions' either.

In the first place, the study of religion is inevitably revealing of the student. If it does not reveal an attitude (positive or negative), it reveals an evaluation of the reality or power of the phenomenon or, if the freedom to prioritize is absent, of the very lack of such a choice.

In the second place, students of religion are required to use their subjectivity as one of their major tools, for individual religiosity can no more be excluded from the phenomenon as a whole than it can be equated with it. Phenomenology in religion means entering into the religious experience of the subject because the object of study is, in part, itself subjective. (To distinguish it from that collection of data and comparison of types which marked Religious Education in Britain in the 1970s, the latter might better be called 'phenomenality': it fought shy of exploring the inner, subjective 'logics' of the human phenomena.) In Religious Studies the entomologist, so to

41

speak, is also a drama student: (s)he enters into the butterflies (s)he displays (cp. Grainger, 2001). Failure to do so means becoming less, not more, than human. Success means becoming both more aware of differences and therefore more catholic at the same time.

However, all that is required is to revise the issue. For, on the one hand, that which is 'personal' (in the sense of individual and/or private) cannot and should not be discussed in general terms and/or in public and, on the other hand, that which is set forth quasi-impersonally should be met on its own terms. The therapist, prophet or guru may (should) ignore the ratiocination, question the questions and name the motives. As student of religion, the scholar must begin with the material presented and (true to his/her profession) be prepared to draw any or no conclusion as to what is the heart of the 'matter'.

The reaction of students of religion to their particular problems in gauging transcendence sometimes seems to elide into 'explaining' the evidence which they are committed to exploring and then into 'explaining away' its distinctive character as religious. This 'elision' can take the form of finding 'explanations' of a historical, social or psychological nature and finding parallels between contingent, structural or personality factors and religious developments and then assuming that consonance equates with causality, in one direction alone, and ignores the questions raised by the continuing apparent religiosity of the phenomena of the original investigation.

It is his careful avoidance of such elision that makes Max Weber (a holistic student of life as well as of religion) continually talk in terms simply of 'elective affinity'. *The Protestant Ethic and the Spirit of Capitalism* (Weber, 1904–5) is as focused and precise in its concepts and analysis as in its data and causal hypothesis: the essay no more equates Protestantism with causing capitalism than (horror of horrors) it equates the 'Protestant ethic' with the 'work ethic'. Weber's ability to maintain such distinctions may be not uncon-nected with his prolegomenon that he was, religiously, 'tone-deaf'. Perhaps (Buddha-like?) his freedom from religious stances (including anti-religious positions) facilitated such discernment.

Whatever may be thought of any metaphysical implications, the ontological status of religion as a source of ultimate categories should not be ignored. No doubt Durkheim spoke for and to his time, with its collector's discovery of evolution, in providing a scientific myth based upon ethnography. However, we have only to look at current language to gauge the place of religion in facilitating the description and communication of dichotomous extremes (Bailey, 1990a).

The widespread apprehension of religiosity as fundamental to that which is distinctively human, and climactic in it, is no doubt responsible for the ever growing, yet rarely remarked, overlap or borrowing of concepts between analyses of religions and those of society. Examples in scholarly and/or popular usage, include: absolve and agnostic, abracadabra and acolyte, apocryphal and apocalyptic, apostle and apostate, alpha and omega, Armageddon and atone, angelic and aisle; Bible and blessed, baptise and bishop; charisma and cult, calling and cow and cabal, Church and communion, confession and creed, canonical and cure, collegiate and cathedral, convert and catechize, curial and catholic; divine and diabolical, disciple and discipline, doctrinal and dogmatic, David and Jonathan, Daniel and the lion's den; Eden and exodus, evangelistic and epitaph; fellowship and funeral, fundamentalist and fury; God and grave, gift and guru, genesis and grace; hell and heaven, hermit and hagiographical, *hocus pocus* and hair shirt, high priest and holy of holies; intone and idolize, iconoclast and inquisitor; Job and Jeremiah, Judas and Jonah, Jew and Jerusalem; kenotic and kiss of peace; latter-day and last judgement, lament and Lazarus; Mary and Martha, Mahatma and Moses, Methusaleh and myth; Noah's ark and the flood, novice and neophyte; orthodox and ordained; *pax* and pious, *potlach* and pilgrimage, parochial and pastoral, pulpit and pew, pope and priesthood, Pilate and pharisee, pillar and prelate, preaching and penance, puritan and prayer, person and pious; religion and ritual, rubric and regular; sacred and sacramental, symbol and sin, sect and service, sermon and Swiss Guard, sanctuary and shibboleth, sacrifice and scapegoat, soul and secular; taboo and temple, theology and trinity; unction and unctuous; virtue and vice, voodoo and vow; witch doctor and worship. (No doubt a glance through a dictionary, or through an encyclopedia of religion, could fill in the alphabetical gaps and provide many other examples, especially from other than the Judeo-Christian tradition, in non-Western languages.)

Their witness to the (Durkheimian) function of religion, as a source of types and categories for the experience as well as the object of human consciousness, is in no way diminished, either by their occasional misuse, or their sometimes avowedly metaphorical status, or by their possibly secular origin, or the ambiguity of their primary reference, or by their inclusion of a degree of humour or hostility. As religion itself becomes less imperialistic in a post-modern world and its perception becomes less threatening, so its utility increases as a model for understanding the distinctively human, including secularity and its autonomy. When the cosmos is primarily cultural and existentially plural, the gods are more easily seen as empirical, ubiquitous, and inevitable. (p. 210)

Such descriptions, using such categorizations, would not make sense to the speaker, let alone communicate to the audience concerned, were the religious not an experience that was itself known, if only indirectly. Such 'religious experience' is too easily equated with momentary experiences of transcendence such as those described by William James in *The Varieties of Religious Experience* (1902) and by subsequent students of conversion experiences, when the subjects have exhibited self-transcendence. Yet the reader of the Psalms or of the Philokalia (let alone a Sufi, guru or Zen Master) might wonder at the uncritical acceptance of such self-confessed conversion experiences and the restricted range of the religious experiences described as 'varied'. It is difficult (although apparently possible) to deny any significance whatsoever to all overnight conversions or momentary revelations, but it is impossible, to judge by public parlance, to avoid giving some meaning to religion, at least in this broader sense.

To restrict the meaning of 'religious' experience to the temporally short-lived is to restrict it to the dramatic, different and unusual. In small-scale contexts this may be simply an intense experience of the usual. All bushes 'burn' in some degree but we don't always 'see' it. In large-scale societies, with their 'impersonal' cosmos, it results in restricting 'real' religion to the sectarian group or ghetto and the contra-natural miracle. The 'Noanic' Covenant, as against the Mosaic Covenant, however, apparently embraced the whole of the human species (at least) and declined to divorce natural law from the moral law. Japanese religious studies and Southeast Asian anthropologists, such as Geertz, seem to lead the way in working with these various 'levels' for other 'sizes' of religion simultaneously: as Chinese boxes rather than stages of linear development. A subjective (as against an emotional) understanding of religion allows us to see both intense faith and relaxed peace (the holy and the human) as religious – as the ends of a continuum rather than of a see-saw.

More will be said on this subject in Chapters 4 and 5. For the nub of the problem is the relation of religion to the human (as a species). Is religion a time-bound, culture-specific, historically-finite phenomenon or is it a dimension of human being (like sexuality)? Does the error lie with those who see specific forms of religion as typological, or with those who see the term's extension as mere metaphor (or even as special pleading)?

Postlude: changing meaning

It might be asked why more has not so far been said, in a volume in a series entitled *Issues in Contemporary Religion*, about the kind of issues discussed at the Annual Methodist Conference that was reported on the BBC's Radio 4. The constant importance today for those with religious responsibilities of questions like the four that were mentioned cannot be gainsaid: the nature of believing, let alone the content of belief; failing to respond to the plethora of opportunities and needs, let alone keeping the existing organizations afloat; the reaction to such simple blessings as health and affluence, leisure and pleasure, let alone standard moral conundra such as the use of alcohol; and the desire to communicate the style as well as the content of the message, without the media pursuing their own interests in the legitimation of the Lottery. The separate sciences of religion (the collective French noun *réligiologiques* [G. Menard, 1990–] may be a better title) already have a wealth of fascinating and illuminating knowledge and insights to share from such perspectives as biology and demographic studies, economics and social studies, history and theological studies.

Such approaches, however, smack rather of 'issues *for* religion' and 'issues *of* religion' than of issues *in* religion. Practitioners, leaders and students of religion are daily aware of their existence. Having observed them all, 'from [their] youth up' in some cases, they have the further issues, 'Which is the greatest of them all?' and, faced with so many offers of help, 'What must I do to gain eternal life?', i.e., 'Where do my real priorities lie?'

The title 'Issues *in* Religion', however, indicates a desire to focus upon the phenomenon itself, rather than upon its manifold aspects. Whatever else religion also is, it is in some sense or senses 'personal'. The religion of the later Roman republic may initially seem formal, mechanical and remote but that was the 'official' religion or, better, the religion of the 'official' sector within a wider framework of religion. To equate the Vestal Virgins, the geese and their sacrifices, with the entirety of Roman religion might be akin to equating the

45

Latin orations at the conferment of honorary degrees by Oxford University with the whole of British formal education, let alone with all that is learned informally. Other understandings of Roman religion and of Roman life speak of the one permeating the other so much, at every *turn*, as to be a constant factor. The transfer of a piece of land involved over thirty invocations of divinity, according to Max Weber; the gods were equally explicitly encountered daily within the household and every time the threshold was crossed; while the significance of that *ethos* of pietàs, with which such symbolic life cannot have avoided being linked, is a truism.

The meaning of 'personal' (like that of 'religion') changes as the character of 'person-ality' changes. The extent of the change is underestimated, leading to constant mis- (or un-)understanding. The classic example must be the change in meaning between the formulation of the Christian creeds in terms of three 'persons' who were yet one God and the meaning of 'person' following the rise first of modern individualism and then of contemporary subjectivism. Anthropology indicates 'before' either of these stages, however, that 'personality' can be diffused throughout the cosmic environment without being particularly centred in any single organism. 'The globe' *could* not be envisaged as 'dead to me' (Watts, 1674–1748) before Newton. Relatively, the living and the dead, the individual and the group and the cosmos were fundamentally one and all lived or died together.

More will be said of these changes or, better, of this cumulative variety of meanings in Chapters 4 and 5. Meanwhile, it is suggested, one issue in religion is to attempt to maintain the focus on the personal, however that and the religious are expressed, because that is the constantly changing, yet consistent, constituent of religion.

3. Alternatives

Prelude: consensus among the faithful

Contemporary 'issues in religion' were sketched in terms of problems facing practitioners, leaders and students of religion. Some of their reactions to their problems were described as the tendency to deny their identity as practitioners, to maximize the degree of difference between the religious and the secular as leaders, and to ignore some of the evidence regarding the peculiarity of religion, on the part of students. In this chapter we continue with the same tripartite typology.

This is not intended, however, to imply a bounded or even satisfactory division. For instance, the religious leader was also once, and presumably still is, a religious practitioner. Likewise (as has already been indicated of particularly the greatest religious leaders) religious practitioners and leaders at lesser levels are not devoid of observation and analysis of the religious realities around them. Scholars might do worse, for instance, than pay them the degree of attention paid by anthropologists to native commentators upon the society they are studying (as religious leaders are themselves learning to do in more particular ways than those implied by the *consensus fidelium* and *ijma*).

However, to treat these three aspects of religion as divisions would not only deny the degree of overlap, it might exclude from consideration that huge body of people who participate vicariously. Active participants, like their leaders, may not always like it but they speak for such 'passive participants' more than is sometimes realized. They may speak 'for' them, not in the sense of deliberately acting as their representatives, but in the sense of being a more vocal 'straw poll'. They may reflect the *consensus fidelium*, the *ijma*, or they may be as off-centre as the handful of clergy used by the media. This is why people can so easily slip into, and slip out of, both religious practise and religious leadership. Indeed, those who practice without leading in any way and those who for whatever reason cease to lead often alike cease to practice.

This can be interpreted as the disappointment of a mere ego-trip and seen as sounding the death-knell to traditional ideas of the Church *dicens* and *docens* (teaching and learning). Alternatively it can be seen as pointing to a universal human vocation to share in a creativity that is divine. Gone, or going, are at least some of the old forms of 'them' and 'us'. In liturgy, pastoralia and evangelism, as in the theatre, education and shopping, 'engagement' comes through hands-on participation.

It is with a range of such possible alternative reactions to issues in contemporary religion that this third chapter is concerned. Their enumeration might smack of advocacy but they could not be envisaged were they not already in some degree happening. 'Issues *in* religion' requires that among the other factors behind their occurrence, motives of a religious character need to be taken into account. The temporal sequence of these is not fundamental; they may take the form of *ex post facto* legitimation, for instance from the canonical tradition, of that which was in point of fact undertaken spontaneously. Yet in retrospect this itself might be seen as having been inspired by the (unconscious) guidance of the tradition or as moved simply by the spirit of humanity. Whatever the cause(s), these alternative possibilities are presented as some of the ways in which things are going and must go.

1. In general: acknowledging, cooperating, communing

Religiously, the West was noted towards the end of the twentieth century for the growth first of voluntarism and then of pluralism. Some contextualizing and localizing reflections may be offered.

Neither feature is altogether novel. Certainly, people now increasingly choose for themselves the degree to which they identify with their religion and which religion they will identify with (if any). There are said to be places, in rural Greece for instance, where the community as a whole decide who should be ordained priest and where there is only choice between various degrees of accepting or rejecting the one religion rather than choosing between different religions. Likewise, a leading Dutch Humanist has spoken of growing up in the 1950s in a village that may have been Protestant or Catholic, in others' minds, but which saw itself as simply human. Yet such examples are sufficiently esoteric as to attract comment and are assumed to be anachronistic; while ordination itself is increasingly returning from an individual bishop's judgement of another individual's sense of personal calling to being a matter for group discernment. However, many individuals seem to have less rather than more chance to make positive religious choices. Indeed, David Martin suggested (1973) that its intense religious debates made Victorian Britain more truly pluralistic than its twentieth-century descendant.

Moreover, it is difficult to think of a time or place that was altogether without voluntarism. In a sense, religion has always represented the voluntary principle itself. However broadcast the call, positive decisions (to follow a Master, preach the Gospel, join a dedicated community) have always been relatively rare, indicating that 'religion' and 'voluntarism' were identical, at least at the official level. Thus, to be stuck within popular religion was to be (like today's popular secularity [Bailey, 1997b]) 'in thrall to the powers of the world' instead of taking one's destiny into one's own hands. Perhaps the main difference is that recently the regard which once went to the religious now goes to the anti-religious. So one day perhaps the media will be able to exploit the fear inspired by the current secular consensus, just as now they manage still to exploit the fears inspired by the old religious hegemony.

It is likewise difficult to think of a time or place that was altogether without pluralism. History is notoriously replete with religious sects and controversies especially in those contexts, such as the European nation–state, in which uniformity was expected. Yet, insofar as pluriformity was taken for granted, 'peace' of a sort reigned historically in India and China. Where changing one's religion was difficult, as in the Hindu caste system, a renunciation, which was itself religious, was a recognized option open to all (though easier for males). Even Islam, like Christianity, acknowledged the validity of choice between degrees of religiosity. Moreover, as religion increasingly replaces gender, race or culture as the vehicle of identity, and as religions increasingly define themselves as mutually exclusive, it becomes more, not less, difficult for individuals to be themselves pluralistic.

So the future seems to lie in increasingly acknowledging one's religious identity. This is contrary to Luckmann's thesis in his great little book, *The Invisible Religion* (1967). Subtitled *the problem of religion in modern society,* it might have been subtitled 'the problem of identity in modern society'. Disregarding the survivability of the denominations (Edwards, 1969) and the 'ecumenical' change from denomination to global religions, like most prophets in the 1960s, Luckmann underestimated the possible indestructibility of the organized religions and, one imagines, the speed and extent to which his 'invisible religion' would indeed give birth to a more universal 'spirituality'.

It is striking and greatly to his credit that Arnold Toynbee, although not at all religious himself but no doubt under the influence of his life-long *A Study of History* (1933–9), ventured precisely this prediction about identification by religion in *A Historian Looks at Religion* (1961), in the golden summer of secular triumphalism. Only in this way, he suggested, would one either be one's self or gain the respect of others, once nationalism had had its heyday.

Groups like the Women's Institute, who at the beginning of the twentieth century included 'non-sectarian' as an ideal in their 'mission statement', or the Red Cross, who at the end of the twentieth century decided to corporately distance themselves from all religions, begin to seem, at least in this respect, like period pieces. They are comparable, on the one hand, to the Salvation Army with its bonnets and literal belief in the descent of the human race from Adam and Eve or, on the other hand, to the National Secularist Society and Rationalist Press Association, tilting at the windmills of a long-abandoned dichotomous supernaturalism.

We now see that the present is far more religious in any and every sense, for good and ill, than we had recognized. Not only will the future be religious but it will recognize itself to be so. However, it may use the word 'spiritual', for we can never be sure what form the 'religious' will take.

Looking at the problems and even the reactions, this prospect may seem fearful. Yet in two ways it is hopeful. Empirically, it is honest, rather than hiding what it dislikes, and philosophically it is open-ended, rather than placing its faith in a mechanistic system (whether that is seen as destined to succeed or to fail). It allows for the possibility of the spiritual which, whatever else it may entail, must include the unpredictable.

A positive outcome of such public identification by religion may appear a forlorn hope in view of Northern Ireland and the Balkans, let alone the Middle East. Yet it could be achieved by a cooperation in practical matters which does not exclude personal religion but, on the contrary, acknowledges the alterity of the neighbour, enabling cooperation to become the doorway to interpersonal communion. Now that the ecumenical movement has begun to go 'pan-religious', we may hope to see non-governmental humanitarian organizations as contexts for an inter-faith dialogue that is more than merely verbal or social.

2. For specialists: distinguishing, communicating, incorporating

Religious leaders have sometimes reacted to their problems by maximizing the differences between the leaders and the led, between those inside and those outside their 'fold', between the religions themselves or between religion and irreligion. The alternative is not to minimize or deny such differences, any more than it is for religious practitioners to deny their commitments. On the contrary, having confessed their identity, as religious and as leaders, the alternative is to develop their discernment of all such distinctions.

This is already happening, at remarkable speed. So far have we come in the first decade of the twenty-first century that it is embarrassing to consider where we so recently were: English grandmothers in 1961 unable to distinguish conceptually between 'Africans' and Palestinian Arabs, British undergraduates in 1956 hardly able to distinguish visually between Chinese and Indian, Anglican seminarians in 1962 unable to distinguish theologically between Islam and Hinduism. Much of the credit for this educational progress must go to television (which was, educationally speaking, 'secular' and suspect). Similarly, much of the progress in religious sophistication that is now being made is being made, and no doubt will continue to be made, under the auspices of such 'secular' agencies as education and the social sciences.

In the last third of the twentieth century, for instance, spiritual direction, along with pastoral care on the one side and theological ethics on the other, were revolutionized by psychology's conclusion that self-love was a necessary component of, and indeed the essential foundation for, love of anyone and anything else. It is to be hoped that those responsible for revising liturgy have similarly listened to educational analyses of school worship, and ethicists to business studies' analysis of value systems. For the conjunction 'as', in 'Love thy neighbour as thyself', suddenly became symbiotic and positive rather than comparative and critical. In this respect, it might be added, the intelligentsia as a whole were rediscovering and re-evaluating (without, as usual, realizing it) a traditional item within folk psychology, popular ethics and traditional wisdom (Bailey, 1997a: 91–3). Religions other than Christianity may not have experienced the same need to learn this lesson, because their leaders may never have been so distant from their members.

Worship is one area in which leaders of the Christian and any other monotheistic religion might have been thought expert. It was possible in the 1960s, however, to train and be trained for the ministry of the Church of England without even asking, let alone answering, such questions as the 'why' and 'what' of worship as an existential activity rather than a historical repository. Fortunately for the Churches (and in due course for other religions, no doubt), the schools (especially the primary schools), as they 'got out from under' clerical influence (or the fear of it), have rediscovered for themselves the place of creativity in worship and experienced its redemptive power. In Britain, at least, practice has been followed by theory at the instigation, interestingly, of a government which balanced its professed attention to the 'bottom line', with a simultaneous drive to revive worship and religious education in schools and spirituality in education generally. Distinctions were drawn by educationists rather than liturgists, by ministers of state rather than ministers of religion, between corporate worship and collective worship and between theocentric prayer and spiritual education, and so on. While such fundamental beginnings may only be the harbinger of what is to come, it is doubtful whether the Christian or any other religion has yet fully taken them on board. They may, however, illuminate the central issues posed by the existence of religion.

A third area in which alternative reactions are possible, in addition to spiritual direction and worship, is the understanding of the nature and functions of religion itself. The middle third of the twentieth century saw an attempt to distinguish religion of every kind (as a human invention, shield and idol) from Christian faith. Fathered by Karl Barth, the distinction was useful against the Nazis.

However, combined with Luther's 'grace alone' and Kierkegaardian existentialism, it encouraged Lutheran seminarians to evaluate preaching by the *lack* of hearers and English Anglican ministerial training to officially omit ethics. North Atlantic theologians tested its global validity, seeking a place in theology for world religions for the first time since the seventeenth century. The attempt seems to have been hampered by Barth's earlier excessive disjunction between 'faith' (true, Christian religion) and ethics, and by the globalist theologians' tendency to hypostasize the religions (as distinct from culture, society, humanity, life, natural faith and the spiritual).

The definition of religion is indeed problematic. Nevertheless, it is a necessary quest. If religious leaders wish to communicate with others and if they acknowledge that designation at all, they may seek to refine its meaning (as suggested below), but they can no more eliminate its use, as the failure of Wilfred Cantwell Smith's plea (1964) has shown, than they can abolish the phenomenon itself.

However, as just indicated, not only will religious leaders distinguish themselves by acknowledging their identity, like any other practitioners, and refine their distinctions of spiritual realities in order to clarify their understanding of their craft, but they will also seek to communicate. This will, indeed, appear an uphill struggle (as already indicated, with reference to the 'mass' media), but at least their difficulties may indicate that their efforts are well placed. For they will want to change the world's mind: its assumptions, attitudes and ambitions. And they will not be the first religious leaders to have problems in making themselves understood. Indeed, some sort of sacrifice and victimization of the believer, not of those 'innocent' of such belief, seems to be the only possible proof of sincerity, as well as an indication of some degree of success.

However, successful 'communication' is more than a matter of technique (vocabulary, image, structure) alone. Involved in it, in fact as well as in name, is 'communion'. This is one of the consequences of incorporation. Just as we can love our enemies *as* ourselves, so this incorporation enables us to talk to ourselves and thus communicate successfully. Our differences enable us to be saved from ourselves. The alternative to an ego-trip is to be 'rooted in love'.

3. Among analysts: recognizing, reconceptualizing, remodelling

Analysts of religious affairs have the double problem of gauging the transcendent and of exercising empathy without allowing their own position to influence their judgement. They may wonder whether, thus hobbled, they are conducting a wild goose chase in the dark. They nevertheless manage to find at least some golden eggs through their recognition of data of all kinds.

What may have been lacking in the final decade or two of the twentieth century are widespread attempts to formulate general accounts of religion. Hesitation is understandable, for several reasons, but in the 1960s and 1970s a small crop of such 'theories' (Luckmann (1967), Berger, Bellah, Cantwell Smith, Eliade) proved stimulating and enlightening. They marked a welcome return to the period of the 'great explorers' (Martineau, Soderblom, Otto, Durkheim) around the beginning of the century. It may be that those that appeared in the 1980s and 1990s (mainly in the guise of undergraduate texts: see Bailey, 1998a, for a list of examples) were just as creative in themselves but received less attention, partly because of the vagaries of the market. Whatever the case, the time may be ripe for a degree of reconceptualization.

Perverse though it may appear, the process of reconceptualization might begin with the concept of secularization. The term is a favourite of sociologists generally, not just sociologists of religion. Indeed, it can be seen as sociology's charter, legitimating the scientific, non-religious study not simply of religion but rather of society and thus of people. The hypothesis it enshrines (if that is the right word) suggests that religion is declining and that that trend is both spreading and irreversible. 'Religion' can therefore already be proleptically disregarded or regarded as, at best, a temporary epiphenomenon. Sociologists, historians and others in the 1960s (the golden summer of this hypothesis), discussed the meaning of the term at length. There was much insight but less agreement.

Perhaps the answer is that the meaning changes; so a plurality of definitions is legitimate and indeed necessary. Its variability is not, however, arbitrary; it is a dependent variable. For the meaning of 'secular' is dependent upon that of 'religious', to which it is always the opposite. So that, indeed, whenever we know what 'religious' means, it will become obvious what 'secular' means and vice versa.

This slightly perverse methodology may therefore shed light upon an issue of considerable analytical, managerial and practical (as well as legal and fiscal) significance. For instance, we know precisely what 'secular' meant in medieval Western canon law (and still means, in contemporary canon law). It meant (means) 'of the world' or 'worldly', understood temporally and institutionally, rather than spatially (or morally or spiritually). It was used to refer to a person or property that was released from its 'religious' status. This did not mean that the person or item ceased to be religious in the modern sense or was no longer (for instance) Christian. It simply meant that they no longer belonged to the religious Order to which they had belonged. They were now *secular* clergy or *non*-monastic lay people or *parochial* church buildings, etc.

In other words, 'religious' in Western European languages referred to monastic ('religious') Orders (male and/or female). The *Religio* was the Rule (or Canon) of such an Order, classically and supremely that of Benedict of Nursia, d. 573. Gradually and with some reluctance (to judge by one of the twentieth century's leading medieval historians, Dom David Knowles, himself a Benedictine religious) the use of *Religio* was extended, referring first to canons that professed to restore observance of the original Rule, then to canons that professed to return to the spirit of the original, then to reformations of it and, finally (as with the mendicant Orders of Dominican and Franciscan friars, for instance), to Orders that intended to follow the Gospel counsels in a somewhat different way. If they also were considered 'religious', it was because they were acknowledged to have a *Religio* of their own, albeit not the *Religio* of St Benedict.

Such changes of meaning might appear slight to unaccustomed eyes. Yet we do not need to compare them with the differences between football clubs or music groups, about which people become excited today, in order to grasp their medieval significance. We only need compare their institutional arrangements, study their Rules, observe their liturgy, feel their ethos, listen to their postulants or ex-novices to grasp the significance of items (e.g. Barry, 1997; Banham, 1991) that may be ancient but are rarely arbitrary or obsolete. No one would suggest that any two schools, or, presumably, prisons, are alike, especially boarding schools. In religious Orders ways of life are chosen voluntarily and ordered holistically with a view to the sanctification of every deed, word and thought or lack of them: the divinity is (meant to be) in the detail.

Presumably throughout the Middle Ages, people and properties were continually being formally released from their vows and their religious ownership. Other members of the Order no doubt quietly released themselves by walking out, just as possessions were appropriated *de facto* if not *de iure* by neighbouring landowners or marauders. With the Dissolution of the Monasteries in 1535–7 in England, however, and similar trends elsewhere, such secularization occurred on a massive scale. It was, moreover, authorized by statute not canon law. If this too is secularization, then it is of a different kind. The word begins to gain a second meaning.

Such Dissolutions could be and often were legitimated on the grounds that the Orders were failing to observe their Rule. Dis-Ordered and un-Ruly, they were abrogating their difference and losing both their identity and integrity. They had, it was said, only been religious in name, by their profession (of the Rule). In other words, they had become secular in their actual way of life. However, this did not mean that society as a whole was meant to be made secular or the regional Church abolished, as 'secular' has recently meant. On the contrary, Luther saw marriage as itself a 'religious' (voluntary, holistic, ordered) state; Cranmer hoped his morning and evening conflations of the seven monastic offices would be prayed (by the clergy and the laity: the bell was to be tolled) in every parish and the laity themselves become weekly communicants.

The meaning of 'religious', therefore, came to centre upon the territorial Churches of the nation–state and the familial gathering, rather than the gathered congregations of the religious societies. (Something of the older meaning can still be seen in the description of the Quakers as the Religious Society of Friends – rather than as a society of religious friends.) *Pari passu*, to be (made) 'secular' was to be(come) free from this same institutional and territorial Church, which was usually represented (like the nation–state by its monarch) by the local bishop or clergy. The parallel between this system and that of the nation–state and its monarchy can be seen in the 'English' Civil War cry: 'No Bishops, No King'.

Whether this second meaning of 'secular' (as 'non-ecclesiastical') is considered a legitimate extension of the first ('non-monastic') or merely metaphorical may depend upon the right to 'lay down the law for future thought', which we wish to accord to any particular historical moment. Likewise, our willingness to describe parish clergy and parish churches, for instance, as 'religious' must depend, presumably, upon our estimate of their phenomenological similarity with the erstwhile Religious compared with the difference of form.

We may stick to the canon law definition of each term if we wish, but that could raise the further question whether anyone who is living even in a Benedictine community is truly entitled to be described as a monk (*monachos*, alone). For that term in turn was borrowed from the Greek description of the hermits in the Egyptian desert: they looked to St Anthony, for instance, as their *staretz* (spiritual guide) but lived apart. So the custom of extending the application of terms, according to the inner meaning of the word and of that to which it refers, seems to predate Benedict himself.

Extension or metaphor, monastic and/or ecclesiastical, it seems fairly clear that, although both of those uses survive and to some extent thrive, some kind of third use is now prevalent. What that may mean will be examined below. Meanwhile we may note the context in which it typically occurs: 'I read the papers religiously'. Conversely, following our crablike methodology, it may be possible to establish what 'religious' characteristically means in this third context, by examining what 'secular' means. But there we draw a blank, because, although it is understood, it is hardly ever used in ordinary speech. Once we have rethought our concepts, however, we may be in a better position to remodel the relationship of 'religious' to 'secular', and also to 'profane', and all three of them to ordinary life.

Postlude: Durkheim's 'sacred'

A cleric setting out on the study of religion, in contrast to theology, as a prolegomenon to converting 'implicit religion' from a hunch to a hypothesis, may have felt Durkheim's *The Elementary Forms of the Religious Life* (1947) to be unanswerable with respect to the 'existence' of God, but may nevertheless still feel uneasy with its apparent description of the phenomenology of the sacredness. Defining religion, by implication as though it had a monopoly of the sacred, he rightly polarizes the sacred and the profane, but seems to suggest, at various points, that all that is not sacred is *ipso facto* profane as though that were coterminous with secularity. It must seem foolish to criticize such a basic text but it could be that the relative neglect of so much of human experience by this model may indicate that others, too, have found it less appealing than that oft-quoted initial definition of religion and his subsequent support for his primary aim of insisting upon the inclusion of the social dimension in religion (as in the rest of human life).

His definition of religion runs: 'A religion is a unified system of beliefs and practices relative to sacred things, that is to say, things set apart and forbidden – beliefs and practices which unite into one single moral community called a Church, all those who adhere to them' (1947: 37).

The implication of the definition, and of the subsequent text, is that religion is based upon the apprehension of the sacred, apparently *without remainder* on either side of the equation. This may be a satisfactory description of what he wishes to call religious in the life of aborigines. Their closest concept may have been 'the dreaming' (Stanner, 1963). However, he did not wish to confine his account to 'visions' (as some North American peoples' studies did) or to 'liturgy', 'ritual' or 'worship', which might have allowed him to equate religion with a (socially-induced) sacred. Yet it is a curious equation. On the one hand, he might have hesitated to call everything that was associated with religion in the France of his day 'sacred' and, on the other hand, he left no room for anything in aboriginal life to be sacred, if it was not also religious.

However, it is the functioning of his model rather than the dynamics of his definition that causes the greatest unease. In the first place, it is encouraging to see the 'profane' included in a discussion of religion. The Devil (or devils) may or may not have a place in theology (or 'angelology'), but the place of abhorrence in religious experience and study would seem to be as obvious as that of awe or reverence. As a negative religious emotion, it belongs with its polar opposite, as 'hate' is twinned with 'love'. At the opposite end of the same spectrum, it belongs in the same category. It is comparable to the taboo, which is an inevitable consequence or inherent part of the attraction that is exercised by the sacred.

In the second place it is surprising to find all that is 'outside the temple' described as profane. With his 'profane', as with other scholars' *Religio*, simply to rely on what can only be a hypothesis regarding the etymology of a word in classical Latin, in order to decipher the meaning of a kindred contemporary term and the significance of the phenomenon to which it refers, is a remarkable short cut. It assumes that the suggested etymology, whether modern or classical, is semantically correct. It assumes that the classical understanding of the phenomenon itself is correct. It assumes that the meaning of the term and the significance of the phenomenon have remained unchanged for millennia (despite the changes in the structures of which they are a part). It assumes that the ancients' putative understanding of a particular phenomenon within their own context is applicable to phenomena that are putatively similar both in significance and/or appearance, even in the aboriginal and/or contemporary context.

Third, it takes no account of the potential ambiguity of intention present within the original Latin. Durkheim's English translator suggests that he takes *pro fanum* to mean 'outside the temple' but a more literal and accurate translation would be 'before the temple'. However, the offering that is before the temple and the one carrying it may be static, or they may be passing by the temple, accidentally or purposely 'on the other side'. Alternatively, they might have just emerged from the temple, either in high dudgeon or with their sanctification completed. Or, yet again, they could be on their way into the temple – they are, after all, before it. And even if they had no such intention, they could still feel themselves sanctified by others' offerings or by the simple presence of the temple in their midst. (For a similar rainbow of possible meanings, in this case regarding a partition in a church-cum-community centre, see Bailey, 1969: 38–9.)

The apparently peculiar dependence upon a simple etymology is, it seems, matched by a similarly peculiarly simple phenomenology of the profane. That and the slide from 'categorial' to 'categorical' opposition between sacred and profane account for the fourth *lacuna* in the model: the absence of the ordinary. For most people, most of life is not particularly sacred or profane. It may be just a little sacred or hardly sacred at all: it is, broadly speaking, relatively (but not completely) secular.

The last apparent gap in Durkheim's model of the religious and the sacred/profane, then, is the absence of that reciprocity between the sacred/profane on the one hand and the ordinary/secular on the other, which gives much of life its dynamism. For, like thunderstorms, battles may sometimes be seen as taking place between the heavenly forces of good and evil; but most strife, like the weather, is earthbound. It is the function of the sacred to relate to that humdrum, sanctifying it and challenging it, representing it and moulding it, which in turn qualifies and defines the sacred. Yet this is hardly apparent in Durkheim's account of it, except in his account of the origin of categories.

The implications are far more than merely theoretical. Equating the sacred with the religious and defining the sacred as 'set apart' from life, as Church sometimes is from State and religion from society, he cannot see much hope for humanity, once the rose-tinted spectacles are off and this understanding is adopted. Others, both ecclesiastically religious (e.g. W. S. F. Pickering) and otherwise (e.g. B. R. Wilson), have adopted approximately his analytical distinctions and drawn similarly pessimistic conclusions.

Part II
Religion in Three Dimensions

4. A three-dimensional model of religiosity

Prelude: the need for three dimensions

'Religiosity' used not to be a very popular term. Usually it carried overtones of an untoward display of religious feeling, indicating a lack either of balance or of sincerity. In this way it was similar to 'pious' and 'piety'. But some term seems necessary so long as 'religion' either refers primarily to the institutional expression of religion or, referring to both inward and outward forms, fails to pinpoint the experience of religion, which is what is intended here. 'Religious experience' would be a viable alternative, although slightly longer, except that it is still customary to use it to refer to particular and specific, short-lived religious experiences, whereas what is intended here is both long-term experience of religion and ordinary experiences that have a religious character, whether brief or long-lasting (cp. Dupré, 2002). However, the growing use of religiosity gives it the kind of neutrality which piety now enjoys, at least in formal Religious Studies.

The model of religiosity that forms the core of this volume is meant to be 'three dimensional' in more ways than one. First, it is meant to reflect reality and to work rather than being a paper-thin drawing, a mythical stereotype based on projection. It is meant to feel right, to feel like the real thing. Second, it is meant to place on a single continuum three experiences whose currently conceptualized relationship seems flawed: the sacred, the secular and the profane. Third, it is meant to bring together social scientific, historical and religious studies approaches. Finally, it finds that 'religion', in the sense of experience which can be accessed phenomenologically (the religiosity that characterizes the distinctively religious), has three forms and that *all three are necessary, to understand both its current use and the phenomenon itself.*

1. Social experience: ecology, society, culture

John Donne's 'No man is an island' was written in 1624. Its recent popularity is as significant as the date of its composition. His images may reflect the recent geographical discoveries and developments in cartography. But he was putting an old message in a new form. Throughout the Middle Ages, society had been portrayed in the form of a human body, drawing upon Paul's image of the presence of Christ in the Church (and in creation).

Before the seventeenth century was out, Donne's fellow-countryman, Thomas Hobbes, saw society as the consequence of agreement rather than inheritance, contract rather than nature, human rational choice rather than divinely willed creation. No doubt his image in turn reflected the experience of the settlers in, rather than discoverers of, North America and the constitutional arrangements (their corporate rule or *religio*) that some of them made, before setting sail in order to maximize their freedom. In the Middle Ages freedom usually meant the liberty of a civic community or professional class: now it increasingly refers primarily to individuals, seen in the context of nuclear family and near neighbours.

The North American novelty has gradually become the norm, at least of the Western world. A Socialist or Labour Prime Minister, Harold Wilson, in the 1960s revived the concept of the Social Contract not as a minimalist expression but in order to stress that individuals should think in terms of obligations at all. A Tory or Conservative Prime Minister, Margaret Thatcher, in the 1980s famously said, 'There is no such thing as society, only individuals', though immediately, no doubt for the sake of 'common' sense as well as political reasons, contradicted herself by adding 'and the family'.

It is in this context that sociology developed as a scientific study and the concept of society as something other than a large, coherent, living body gained ground. As a category, such societies approximated to the Western European nation–states. Each was a relatively self-contained military, economic, linguistic, cultural and religious unit. The category was suspiciously small but the spread from

Western Europe of a nationalism that was sometimes little different from a romanticized corporate tribalism confirmed its propriety and growth. North American steps towards the 'thickening' of society proved a natural focus for such mechanistic analysis.

As well as the breakdown of the medieval corporatist view of society and the rise of the nation–state society, a third factor is relevant in this context: secularization. This has sometimes been of the first type mentioned in Chapter 3: a member of a religious order who has been canonically secularized (or, if ordained, has left the priesthood) and thus changed their 'profession' (for instance, to sociology). Some have discontinued active participation in the Church also, some have either concentrated upon, or else renounced, the study of religion. For a mixture of reasons, few have publicly drawn much upon their past profession.

For this reason if no other, therefore, it is the second meaning of secularization that has come to the fore. This is concerned not with the status of individuals or material possessions in canon law, but with the standing of professionals and their professional institutions *vis-à-vis* the territorial Church in civil law.

In the eighteenth and nineteenth centuries supremely in Western Europe, and in the twentieth and twenty-first centuries in developing nations elsewhere (beginning with the USA), the issue has focused on such questions as, on the one hand, the continuing rights and responsibilities of the Churches as the founders (often) of educational institutions, and the place of the Church, the Christian faith and religion as a whole in the national education system, and, on the other hand, the right or responsibility of the teacher or student to intellectual or ethical autonomy. The questions are particularly Roman Catholic issues because that Church has placed greatest stress on formal institutions and central control. However, it is paralleled in Orthodox unease over the boundaries between the Church and the nation or tradition and custom, Anglican discussions of the difference between religion and culture, ethics or ethos, and Protestant debates regarding 'the faith' as 'delivered' and faith as experienced.

Sociology was among the new professions, activities and institutions to appear during this time. As the Roman Catholic sociologist, Andrew Greeley (1973) has remarked, almost every new form of institutionalized activity, such as banking, voting and manufacturing, that has developed since 1600 has developed independently of organized religion. However, sociology was not just another such activity. In one way it was less important in the ongoing struggle than, say, banking, because it carried less traditional symbolic value: the Church had long taken note of usury (as Islam still does). In another way, however, it was more significant: it may not have been exactly the flagship of a secularist struggle against ecclesiasticism, in the way that schools and colleges could be, but it based itself on the premise and promise of secularity, supplying the evidence of the cultural process.

The desire to be seen as a 'natural' type of science, the sheer 'faith' in the possibility and value of 'objectivity' in study of the human, and the insistent claim to neutrality could be seen as structural tell-tale: 'Methinks she doth protest too much'. For even the Papacy can only say, 'There is no question' (of ordaining women to the priesthood, for instance), if in fact there is such a question. There have been and are many profound (the word is indicative) sociologists with religious worldviews, but for many, inside and outside the profession, theology was at best a primitive, confused and confusing form of sociology. As on a see-saw, the rise of one required the fall of the other.

The significance of this third factor, secularization, in the background to sociology in particular and the social sciences in general, is borne out by an oft-remarked characteristic of its and their development: the attention paid to religion by the Founding Fathers and its relative neglect since. The Fathers spoke for and to their contemporaries in considering religion. To have ignored it would have constituted a symbolic, indeed deliberate, statement: a value judgement rather than an empirical description, resulting from a quasi-historical prediction at best.

The alleged subsequent 'neglect' of religion by sociology (and by psychology, if not anthropology) similarly reflects its times, but it is significant rather than symbolic. The silence tends to speak volumes but in spite of and because of not trying to make any sort of statement. For it is now possible to live one's life in society without really noticing religion. Indeed, it often seems strange that it receives the attention that it does. Sunday is almost a duplicate Saturday, for instance, the Churches' concern for the family (which defeated the United Kingdom Government on the first occasion) eventually being outflanked (apparently) by that of the retailers.

A third type of secularization has now emerged therefore. If 'Freedom' be taken as their common theme for the moment, the concept is used with the same liberality as that which allows the 'freedom' of a city, which in the Middle Ages meant freedom to incorporate and escape the attention of local barons, to be bestowed upon individuals today as an honorary membership, devoid even of membership charges. If 'freedom' be granted such freedom, the first type of secularization can be described in terms of freedom from adherence to a religious Rule once voluntarily professed. The second type of secularization can be described as freedom from ecclesiastical rule, originating usually in the purposes of the foundation of the institution voluntarily joined. If secularization is considered an appropriate description of this third type of freedom, the question arises of what it is freedom from. Is it freedom from all control, except (presumably) of some secular kind? Such an answer seems not only unlikely but also circular.

Perhaps the time has come to return to the drawing board whence the terms originated. Examining them in their earlier contexts, we may ask whether there is a danger of either using them too narrowly and taking them too literally or else of stretching them too far and using them too loosely. There may be a danger of falling between the two stools of sociological fundamentalism and literary metaphor. Yet that phenomenological position could be precisely where we should be, if we are going to be true to the data themselves.

Religious Studies might be pardoned if it sees sociology as positing a pair of concepts from the start: religion and society. Social Studies might be pardoned if it posits a pair of concepts but gives priority to the one it sees as having the more certain ontological status: society and religion. Indeed, for a variety of reasons (to avoid argument as to their relative status and the nature of their relationship), it may prefer to omit the second term and concentrate on other issues, which admittedly are legion.

However, it could be that the original pairing throws light upon the concept of society and that itself might be illuminating. For society has been seen as having taken three basic forms, often referred to as small-scale society, historical society and contemporary society. This model has usefully extended the horizons of social study but now it may be in danger of focusing attention upon subsidiary aspects of social reality, when better images are available. Thus small-scale societies are less societies, as North Atlantic sociology knows them, than ecologies. That is almost definitional of their character, even of their nature, certainly of their survival on a year-to-year basis.

Likewise, 'contemporary society' or 'mass society' or 'post-industrial society' is difficult to characterize, not only because there is so much of it and we are so close to it, but because it is not 'a society' among other such societies. So it is far from clear that it can any longer, indeed, be accurately (i.e. as an empirical assessment, not as a critical judgement) referred to as a 'society' at all. It may contain societies, as indeed did historical societies, but again they too may be of a different kind. Some see it simply as an economy. However, a better image, directing attention to its more salient human features, might be presented if it were renamed, say as 'contemporary culture'.

If 'religion and society' or 'society and religion' were the Romulus and Remus or, better, the Jacob and Esau at the birth of sociology, and if the threefold typology of small-scale, historical and contemporary societies now require renaming in terms of ecology, society and culture, in order to focus attention on the human component in each situation more appropriately, then the immutability of the 'religion' component is similarly called into question. Indeed, whatever the suitability of applying the concept of 'society' backwards and forwards, so to speak, to small-scale and to contemporary situations, it is noticeable that the applicability of 'religion' to each of those contexts is already under question. 'Religion' becomes myth and ritual, for instance, in the former case, and now frequently becomes 'spirituality' in the latter. Before exploring the implications of such changes, however, and suggesting new formulations, it may be advisable to ponder some of the changes in the form of human consciousness as a whole that are experienced in these different contexts.

2. Human consciousness: intensification – bifurcation, individuation – interrelationship, conscientization – contextualization

A practical issue in contemporary religion is the daily question of prioritizing: what to concentrate on. It is a perennial problem for the religious practitioner, leader or student alike. Affecting all human beings, it increasingly presents itself to those living in contemporary culture, with its relative paucity of traditional compulsions and its plethora of competing opportunities. The leader will share the inevitability of choice experienced by the disciple, but will also ask what the organization, institution or community should spend its time, resources and energy on.

Admittedly the freedom of manoeuvre is limited: the total number of Christian clergy in Britain, for instance, declined by a half during the twentieth century, while the population doubled. And while many of the old religious and social expectations have also declined, new ones have appeared, so that the loss of the freedom to choose increases the need for principles by which to select. The student of religion is in a very similar predicament: if we listen to the practitioners (who might be presumed to know something about it), there is nothing in life that is not in some way connected with religion. Where, therefore, should (s)he begin – or end?

Practitioners, at the intersection of two extremes, may want to know their particular place in the universe; leaders (as leaders) may want to know (as part of their job description) their religious place in society; analysts (*qua* analysts) may conclude the core question concerns the place of the religious within human consciousness.

It may be possible to conduct a magisterial survey of the scholarly study of religion but that would leave untouched much of the oral traditions of humanity, let alone the unverbalized aspects of the remainder of symbolic life. Instead, we may start with Durkheim's *The Elementary Forms of the Religious Life* and justify what may seem like an arbitrary choice of a 'text' by its continuing repute, and its apparent relevance in the leadership of a small group of religious practitioners. From that *magnum opus* we select one theme only. We also widen its description of the particular mechanism employed by Australian aborigines by paraphrasing it so we can pinpoint the principle which Durkheim sees at work. So, instead of restricting our view to 'ritual frenzy', we consider 'sociality' as inclusive of both the external means and the internal consequence. So the resulting 'primary law' of human consciousness runs: the intensification of consciousness and its resultant bifurcation hinge upon a sense of sacredness which is basic to all subsequent categorization.

This 'primary law' stems from studies of small-scale societies ('ecologies') that were inevitably relatively holistic. A second 'law' arises out of the study of human life, mainly in historical societies. It is consonant with and a natural development of the primary law. It says simply: individuation makes interrelationship possible. Romantic love between teenagers is a paradigmatic example. It takes account of and tries to bring together the repeated observations that are made of the ways in which the human distinguishes itself from first the cosmic and then the animal and in which the individual (even more importantly) becomes an island 'separated' from 'the main'. Such ('psychic') 'independence', conversely, facilitates the development of relationships that are identifiable entities in themselves with their own characteristics.

A third law would seem to characterize consciousness (a concept that is characteristic of this stage) in contemporary 'society' (or culture). In this case the two components seem less like a natural sequence, or the opening up of a complementary possibility, than like a pair of contradictory opposites. In practise they are symbiotic, as before.

Thus the oft-remarked 'American' (and hence 'modern' or futuristic) dependence upon the mechanical, the bureaucratic, the legal and the ideological counterbalances rather than contradicts the equally oft-remarked American fondness for the emotional, the subjective, the spontaneous and the idealistic. This 'third law', then, says: conscientization and contextualization require each other. In other words, Marx and Freud (with all they represent) belong together. To understand others and what they say, we enquire not only where they are 'coming from' and 'are at' but also 'what's bugging them', 'eating at them' and 'got into them'.

Both the material quest and the mental quest allow for infinite regress and progress ('that happened because . . .', and, 'you say that because . . .'). Infinity, like ontology, is a vertiginous, quasi-religious experience as well as a theo-mathematical concept. So, in the nature of things, or at least of the mind, it is hard to conceive what form a 'fourth stage' of consciousness might take. It seems more likely that it would (will) result in amending the contents of some similarly tripartite structure. The human mind may have a continuing propensity for triplicity but contemporary consciousness measures worth more by fit-ness (expressive functionality) than by function (survival) or longevity in the manner of its predecessors. So, to say this model is 'offered' rather than 'final' is merely to make a virtue out of a blatant necessity.

3. Religious experience: sensing, encountering, committing

As already mentioned, the 'religious experience' that matters most in the context of 'ordinary religion' is not that of Mother Julian, with her Thirteen Revelations of Divine Love on 13–14 May 1334, or even that of the myriads of our contemporaries, some of whose accounts form the data base of the Alister Hardy Research Centre in Oxford. The kind of religious experience which comprises a religious issue for the majority of people, who are not specialists in theology, psychology or philosophy, is the religiosity of every day life. All kinds of religious experience may be experienced in the course of ordinary living but this kind lacks the dramatic contrasts associated with experiences of momentary transcendence.

It is, therefore, easily overlooked and easily forgotten even by its subject. However, that does not mean it is unimportant. Our wedding breakfast may be a memorable occasion. By contrast our ordinary breakfasts may merely merge into each other, yet they do get us to work. The religion of everyday life may in any particular case turn out to be sheer devotion to the routine itself or, upon investigation, to be devotion to some other end to which our ordinary life is a means or of which it is an expression. Whichever it is, it is that religiosity that keeps us going (the faith that stops us committing suicide, as Tolstoy said) and it is that religiosity with which this volume is primarily concerned.

Three kinds of social experience have been painted: that of an ecology, of a society and of a culture. They were portrayed, as they first appeared, largely as stages in a linear development. With static and impersonal (almost mathematical) models tending to displace dynamic and unpredictable (quasi-historical) stories, as the myths of the modern mind, such figures come naturally to mind and, in certain contexts, communicate readily. An explanation of this model's use is necessary, however, if it is to work effectively.

Thus, although an outline history of social development provided material for the model, its chief function lay in providing the ingredients. It stands or falls on the fitness of the model for the tasks to which it is applied, rather than upon the accuracy or adequacy of the history. Indeed, such a thumbnail sketch could hardly contain enough to be worthy of contradiction.

The first of the points regarding its application, then, is that the three stages may be presented as successive ages in the story of social development, but they are seen rather as three types of social experience. They therefore follow in some sort of sequence but they do not replace one another. (Comparison could be made with the seven days of creation in the opening chapter of the Hebrew scriptures.) They all continue to coexist, side by side, not just across the contemporary globe but within any society (culture) that has reached the third stage, for instance.

Not only are there first and second type societies within contemporary culture: members of contemporary culture themselves migrate, daily, between these types of social experiences. Stereo-typically, adults may kiss their partner goodbye, board a train and greet colleagues at work, and so, in the course of an hour, move from a type one setting, through type three and into type two. The differences in the kind of society experienced can be seen in the manner of expressing the relationships involved: from 'Goodbye, love' (an expletive, describing a particular relationship without needing to name its object), through a numbered ticket (with name, signature and photograph, if a regular commuter), to collegial greetings by personal name.

Second, the sketch, in its historical format, might be tentatively applied to individual as well as social development. Stereotypically, we begin life in that smallest-scale society of all: in the womb and then on mother's knee. An increasing number now move on to playgroups, schools and voluntary interest groups, where they undergo the processes associated with historical societies, becoming literate, beginning to specialize, gaining individualistic identity and learning to relate. Around puberty they then proceed to larger institutions, learn objective ways of thinking, decide for themselves, choose friends. Again the terms of address exactly illustrate the various forms of social experience: from mother's 'Darling', through the single (individual or family) name, to the numbered ID or credit card.

With individual as with social development, there is no reason to equate the three stages with three ages that are successively abandoned. 'The child *is* [not *was*] father to the man', we may insist. 'Men are only little boys in long trousers.' At Christmas, and on the beach, many fathers only need the license to play again like children. If such comments are less common regarding females, it could be because they are less 'staged'.

The three types of social experience outlined are each character-ized by their own distinctive type of consciousness then. Within that consciousness is a distinctive type of religious experience. For the moment, this will be described in experiential rather than substantive terms.

'Ecological' social experience, as typified by the tribe or the baby but regularly experienced in the more intimate forms of ongoing social and individual life, is characterized by an intensification of consciousness that leads to its bifurcation. Religious experience, like other experience, in that context can best be described as sensing, but not in the sense of the five senses, or as feeling, but not as distinct from thinking.

'Historical' social experience, as typified by the city– or nation–state and by the growing child or teenager or by those recurrent contexts in which we are not just a name, is characterized by individuation and interrelationship. Religious experience in that context can be described as 'encountering'.

'Cultural' social experience, as typified by the airport terminal or recorded instruction and situations of virtual anonymity, is characterized by the simultaneous conscientization and contextualization of that consciousness. Religious experience in that context can be described as 'committing'.

A present participle, in the active form, has been used at this point to describe the character of the religious experience in each of the three cases. This seeks to avoid moving too quickly on to the 'content' of experience itself. This 'experiencing' could be seen as the distinctive concern of religious studies, as against theology, philosophy or sociology.

For whatever reason, however, without some attempt at sketching the putative content of the experience, it is difficult to grasp the character of the experience itself. The noun is necessary to give precision to the verb. Attitudes vary and it is certainly easier (and may be necessary) to see them as dependent variables; in other words, as responses. What they are responses to will likewise vary but they are alike in being able to evoke a response.

Postlude: being personal three ways

This threefold model of consciousness, based in social experience and giving rise to different types of religiosity for instance, has numerous other applications. They seem both enlightening and liberating. Apart from any value such a model may possess for understanding human life, such descriptions will immediately alert the student (or the practitioner) of religion, in the East or West, to discard their clodhoppers in order to 'see' the experiences evoked by such a myth. *Theoria* rather than theory, they seem to be of holistic (world-view and attitudinal) value and, therefore, of specific, practical importance. Be that as it may, the model can at least serve as material for the case study of a new religious movement: an example of Troeltsch's cult, albeit with a membership of one.

To take an example with virtually universal application: the widespread comment and complaint that 'modern life is impersonal'. The critics' language is pre-postmodernist: in terms of this model, they are referring to identification by number, communication by recording, assessment by postal code, service by classification, discrimination by category, judgement by stereotype. Most must at some time likewise have bewailed, '*O tempora, O mores*', and similarly wondered, 'Where is it all leading?'

Yet many will also have known for themselves what Harvey Cox described in *The Secular City* (1965) as the joy experienced when that same anonymity means liberty. *Anomie* can license creative as well as licentious spontaneity. The self that can thus find expression may be free of the shackles as well as the restraints of others' expectations.

By referring to such a context as 'impersonal', we may conceal from our own view what may sometimes be better described as new ways of being personal. The human spirit will out, like the grass that grows up between the concrete. If we fail to recognize this, we fail to speak to or for a large and growing sector of human experience. Pavement-dwellers may communicate with passers-by in moans but the street urchin, whether victim or virile or both, can be vital. It is a fact of life that there's more to Life than facts.

This tendency to equate an entire aspect of humanity with the form that we know best affects vast swathes of analysis, judgement and (in)action. We too easily assume that to be personal means the same as being individual, until we learn from 'ecologies' that being a person can be a corporate experience (as well as a legal fiction). Equating 'personal' with 'individual' is, inevitably, involved in the point made earlier about the tendency to try and project 'religion' and 'society' onto other kinds of sociality and religiosity and then, if that proves unworkable, to conclude that they are ethnocentric faculties rather than the culture-bound forms in which continuing 'needs' (or potentialities) find expression.

One of many specific ways in which a fundamentalist approach, equating a particular term for a concept with the reality of the phenomenon itself, can hamper thinking, dis-spirit people and confuse policy is 'university'. The modern university is no more a *uni*-versity of *the* truth, than it is a community. However, neither did the universities of the nineteenth century bear much resemblance to their medieval foundations or forebears (Christian, Moslem or Buddhist). It is possible (and en-couraging), however, to see them not as quasi-holistic residential communities dedicated to the pursuit of the (whole) Truth but as portfolios of project-centred conferences dedicated to the pursuit of a succession of particular truths.

Some will ask why the effort should be made to use the same terms; why not simply accept such substitutes as values, world views, identity, even spirituality for 'religion' and retain that word for its continuing historical forms? One immediate answer need not be as cynical as it may sound: to give validity to Religious Studies. True, Religious Studies will lose its wider appeal if it confines itself to the historical forms of religion (Badertscher, 2002), but Religious and Social Studies are now sufficiently distinct for the former to be able to insist that it can see religious-looking features in contemporary culture which invite empirical investigation and comparative analysis (as journalists constantly demonstrate).

However, the similarity of subject-matter goes deeper than that (as Durkheim showed and as the increasing tendency of the social sciences to use religious-sounding terms such as *charisma* or *communitas* suggests). Religious Studies would want to suggest that a bifocal, two-pronged approach to sociality and human being itself sharpens perspective and facilitates identification. It will also want to explain that Religious Studies cannot be true to its own subject matter if it is sectioned off.

Now Religious and Social Studies are no longer so embarrassingly close (both challenging and therefore taboo), we should be able to take account of such object lessons as the material elements within the sacramental actions. Do they not suggest that the dynamic of the sacred is simultaneously to differentially *represent* the secular and, thereby, to coinherently *confront* it? The principle is similar to loving one's neighbour (or enemy) 'as [being involved in] oneself'.

5. The three dimensions of religious experience

Prelude: religious studies as religious

'Religious Studies' has always been a difficult expression, for a university department to adopt for instance. The study of theology has often been part of professional training for Church ministry and been undertaken in institutions that were founded by and corporately committed to a faith position. So, even when the study of theology has been open to students of all faiths, or of no recognized faith, it has been suspected of having a confessional bias and motive. The problem lies not with the suspicion, which is a statement of the obvious, but with the assumption that teachers are incapable of respecting autonomy and that students are incapable of self-defence.

Comparison may also be justifiably made with other faculties, some of whom are avowedly involved in professional studies (law and medicine, traditionally and significantly) and/or faculties such as music and drama that involve both worldviews and lifestyle (which may be as apparent to fellow-students as the wearing of a uniform). 'Religious Studies', then, should cause no offence: to study economics does not suggest necessarily becoming an economist or being economical. Yet the Study of Religion, or occasionally Religion *tout simple*, has often been preferred as a departmental title to allay the suspicion engendered by 'Religious Studies', if only for the sake of peace and quiet.

Unfortunately these harder titles may encourage a hard approach, limited to the harder aspects of the area. For what Religious Studies does allow for is a 'religious' approach to that which is (as some would say) 'truly religious'; an approach which allows (indeed, requires) students to use their own subjectivity (better, 'subjectivities') as part of their methodological equipment (akin to, and involved in, their visual and audial senses or to participation in dialogue). It is the simultaneous desirability, yet danger, of this technology that sustains the perennial discussion, in every context to do with religious education, of the issue of whether religion can be taught, in any form or for any purpose, by those who are not themselves religious or, contrariwise, whether only the non-religious can teach it.

The nub of the issue (and it is paradigmatic) is what is meant by 'religious'. If we take it to mean 'of the organized religions', then the fears are reasonable, not least when based upon worldwide historical experience. That is not to say they are unanswerable. Apart from the *amour propre* of the teacher and the student, it is also possible to point to the indoctrination imparted and imbibed by studies such as medicine and science, which are all the more dangerous for being unconscious and/or vehemently denied. At least Religious Studies, in the narrower sense (of commitment to a particular religion), is up-front. If, however, Religious Studies is understood to include in the definition of 'religion' the 'unorganized' 'religions' of small-scale ecologies (which it usually already does) and if it is understood also to include, by a forwards rather than backwards projection of its originating typology, the unorganized religiosity of contemporary culture, then the complaint about undercover proselytism for any one religion would be met.

It might not overcome the fear, for that is an emotional or spiritual phenomenon, but its rationalization would be answered. Perhaps the only way of communicating the answer in such a way as to be understood would be to include consideration of the underlying 'religion' of the institution itself, as a whole and in its parts. It would comfortably follow the example of the existing provisions for the study of the *philosophy* of science, the *sociology* of politics – and the sociology of sociology.

At every level, then (practice, management and study), religiosity calls for this three-dimensional or triple-core understanding.

1. Its content: the sacred, the holy and the human

The sacred, as every student of religion knows, is that which is special and set apart. However, which of those two is cause and which is effect may epitomize *the* religious issue (the issue of religion itself), but ideologies rush in where scholars fear to tread. The evidence is there, in every religion, including some of those parts of the Old Testament that concern themselves with religion. This is fortunate, students were told in the 1950s and 1960s, because in the industrial society of those days, it was said, 'sacred' was without meaning and the concept was without content because the experience was no longer available.

At the end of the 1960s (November 1968 – May 1969) interviews were conducted with just over a hundred people, aged between fourteen and their seventies, of both sexes, from a wide educational and religious spectrum. I was interested to find out what made people tick and set the scene with the first question: 'What do you enjoy most in life?' Almost as an after-thought, I included towards the end of the schedule (so they would not mistakenly think it a religious survey, in the ecclesiastical sense) a pair of questions that would help them first to locate the evidence and then to translate the experience into words: 'Is there anything you might be prepared to use the word "sacred" of?', and 'What do you mean or understand by "sacred"?'.

To my surprise, the word was very widely understood. It was also understood to mean precisely what the anthropologists and Old Testament scholars said it had meant traditionally. Three answers to the first of the two questions, that directly illustrate the understanding and were selected as representative, ran:

'Each person's own beliefs.'

'To me, Jesus is sacred. Our Lord is sacred – he's the most sacred thing in my life.'

'People talk about sacred places, but I wouldn't use it at all.'

The three answers (from different members of the cohort probably) to the second question ran:

'Something which is personal, which should be cherished, and which you alone have got. This is where I disagree with Western religion's organised sacredness together at a set time on Sunday mornings. The Tibetan monk, and the whole Tibetan nation, were so fantastically devout – they even frowned on civilisation, and the wheel, until 1949.'

'It's a belief in something that is almost untouchable, or something that has got to be revered in some way.'

'Those aspects of life which directly, or indirectly, relate to God.'

The sacred, then, in contemporary society and culture as in historical societies or in small-scale ecologies, would appear to be that which is special and so in that sense set apart and imposing of taboos. It is, nevertheless, that to which we are attached and joined, that with which we identify, that which though different represents, foetus-like, a part at least of our own selves. When the self is only partially distinguished from the cosmos (relative to their later degree of separation), such sacredness or sacreds are inevitably 'sensed'.

Fearing that 'sacred' would evoke little understanding and confident that the schedule as a whole was working well, 'What would you mean or understand by "holy"?', was added, straight after the pair of questions regarding 'sacred'. Again, the term was understood and again with a precision that surprised this student. The three answers chosen as representative of all the major components, to form a cross-sectional picture of the whole, ran:

> 'The "sacred" isn't religious, but "holy" does mean "religious" to me. I could apply it to everybody's religious symbols. But it's not a word I've clarified yet – it just carries the overtones of incense.'

> 'It's very close to "sacred", but again I would understand it in other people's terms. I am impressed by people who are able to see something as holy, such as people who draw strength from a grave. I approve – though my approval is irrelevant, of course – of a personally-felt holiness.'

> ' "God-fearing" – you can't be a "holy" man, apart from religion; it's an attitude.'

The 'holy', then, in contemporary society or culture, as in historical societies, and empirically, if not typologically in small-scale ecologies (as an anticipation, so to speak), seems to be that which is special, like the sacred, but in a more restricted and focused form. It is more 'religious' and so appears in contexts in which religion is a distinguishable 'entity'. It is closely associated with an individuated 'God', with whom we can compare ourselves, whom we (or others) can grow like but from whom we distinguish ourselves, whom we identify ourselves as different *from*. The holy, then, is inevitably 'encountered'.

The aim of the interviews was to discover what people were committed to. The interviews suggested that 'commitment' itself was indeed an overriding characteristic in their life. (A subsequent study [Bailey, 1997a: 193–262] of a suburban community of seven thousand people also affirmed the importance of commitment for its members.) It hypothesized that it might be called the 'implicit [or secular] religion of contemporary society [or culture]'. Between the interviews and the community study, a study was also made of the life of a public house (*ibid*.: 129–92). All three studies seemed to confirm the heuristic value of that hypothesis. The interviews in particular suggested that commitment was the form which religiosity took in contemporary culture. Hence that description of the character of religious experiencing in the third stage.

The single word that best describes the content of that experiencing must be 'human'. This may seem to be in a different category from the earlier 'sacred' and 'holy'. If that is indeed the case, it must nevertheless be accepted and whatever conclusions are required would have to be drawn. However, the difference may be far less than at first appears.

On the one hand, human is a paradoxical term in the interviewees' own minds: Churchill was (in effect) 'gloriously human' ('He had tremendous personality, humour, many talents, ability as a leader') but was also human in the way the term is continuously used ('only human'). Thus, the same interviewee continues about Churchill, '. . . and *at the same time* lots of human frailties, as he was completely and utterly human. We can read about him and chuckle'. The human, then, can be a kind of transcendent anthropophany. It is certainly ineffable. On the other hand, it is necessary to recall Weber's dictum that most religion has always been oriented towards this world, lest we exaggerate the degree of supernaturalism in traditional religion. The characteristic religious experience of contemporary culture, then, is commitment to the human.

2. Its extrapolation: integrity, identity and divinity

Just before the interview schedule was finalized, in the last of the test cases, it was decided to try out a question regarding identity. The author, having just become aware of the significance of the concept, made it the final question, lest its philosophical character spoiled the atmosphere. The contrary proved to be the case. Its first trial was with a petrol pump attendant in his sixties. His response was immediate and totally comprehending: 'Ah, you've got me there. I've been asking myself that for thirty years'. (It was by no means the last time that the search for 'implicit religion' has led to a bridging of the gap, whereby a cerebral culture learns from those 'schooled in the university of life'.)

The popularity of the concept of identity is an index of its ambiguity as a concept which effectually unites a multiplicity of concerns. It also carries with it a broadly positive evaluation, in contrast to the negative evaluations (of bureaucrats, bosses, unions, politicians, the media and so on) whereby communication is established at the expense of a common scapegoat. A human issue, for both individuals and groups, at the practical level, it is also understood at the level of discourse.

Were it not seen to be in some way a 'religious' issue, then the meaning of 'religion' itself would require adjustment. Fortunately, the (organized) religions have tended to see it as a religious issue, both for themselves and for humanity (and the environment). Using this or other terms, practitioners have wrestled with the search for the 'fundamentals' of their faith, leaders with the search for the historical Jesus (or Buddha, and so on), and analysts with the definition of religion in the effort to identify what each of them 'is all [or "on"] about'.

'Identity' can have two basic strands of meaning: we can identify *with* someone or something, or we can identify ourselves as different *from* someone or something. A parallel might be seen with the split in consciousness (the intensification that precedes bifurcation and the individuation that precedes interrelationship) and with the meaning of 'sacred' and 'holy'. The splits are not mutually exclusive in experience but they are distinguishable and their components may coexist in varying combinations.

Parents' relationship with their children, for instance, may veer, on the one hand, from an identification *with*, which feels the child to be sacred, because 'mine' (as our body is inevitably sacred or profane, not only because it is a source of pleasure or pain but because it is 'me') and, on the other hand, an identification *from*, which regards the child as holy because other (and all the more remarkable because surprisingly different from us, its parents). Such a combination may also be present in relationships between adults. The strength of a marital relationship, for instance, might lie in the simultaneous presence, on the one hand, of possession (traditionally a two-way process, in which those who possess can themselves be possessed by that which they possess, their so-called possessions) and, on the other hand, of differentiation. Whether Durkheim's thesis (that the intensification of consciousness lies at the bottom of all distinctions) accounts for religion may be an open question. Its applicability to romantic love (and in marriage guidance) and to nationalism seems clear.

'Integrity' is another term with popular appeal in both senses of that expression: it is widely understood and what it is understood to mean meets with approval. It also applies to both individuals and groups (anything which has identity). It also unites processes which initially appear contradictory. For integration can be either external (*with* other individuals or groups) or internal (*within* the individual self or group).

Identity may be a particular issue for those whose social experience is 'historical', whose consciousness is concerned with individuality and relationships, and whose religiosity combines the holy with the sacred. Integrity, on the other hand, may be a particular issue for those whose social experience is 'contemporary', whose consciousness balances its technology by being simulta- neously both self-conscious and contextual, and whose religiosity consists of commitment to the human. Instant, global, face-to-face communication, for instance, unleashes forces of integration (with any kind of victim, for example), which depend crucially upon the integrity of individual reporters, editors and owners.

Were human issues of such simultaneously cosmic and ethical dimensions not already perceived as 'religious', they would soon be so. As it happens, the religious have long spoken of a 'peace' that is 'without Gentile or Jew' (because subsuming both), and which 'passes all understanding' (because embracing all categories). Thus religious leaders today have readily adopted (and religious practi- tioners have often pioneered) the juxtaposition of the 'integrity of creation' with 'personal integrity', and religious analysts have interpreted today's Green Movement as being as religious as was yesterday's movement for moral rearmament in its heyday.

3. Its intrapolation: bird, worm and mole

Any merit this essay may have for others may lie in its bird's-eye view. If it is generous in generalities, it is miserly in evidence. A commentary arising from observation at a trig-point, it is offered as a series of hypotheses for consideration.

So it is presented in 'sure and certain knowledge' of at least some of its limitations. These include not only the absence of citations of empirical evidence and theoretical analysis but, more importantly, often (no doubt) sheer ignorance of their existence, as well as an incomplete comprehension of much of what has been heard or read. However, if 'amateurs rush in', it may be because 'professionals fear to tread' and so they may at least be provoked to set the record straighter.

Three factors encourage its offering at all. First is the conviction and the experience that viewing secular contemporary life from an implicit–religious perspective adds to our understanding of it, of other people and ourselves and of religion generally, and that this additional aid can be of use for the practitioner, the leader and the student of religion and of life. (That might be described as a bird's-eye view. It can hardly avoid being superficial, pretentious and impertinent.)

The second factor is the conviction that the worm has its own contribution to make. This worm's-eye view has the merit of what the objective sciences might call empirical data or experiential evidence or the subjective sciences might call anecdote (to a large extent the very stuff of lived religion) or story (to a large extent the very stuff of joined-up living). The current essay has presented its author with the opportunity to try and set in order many things that have jostled in the mind during three decades of attempting to combine the three roles of discipleship, ministry and reflection, which for various reasons, including pressures of time and the plethora of opportunities, often tend, almost inevitably, to drift apart, to their mutual loss. But the worm is limited, in too many ways to list (tempted as one is to do so); a myriad such contributions to the general debate are needed and a team to marshall them.

The third factor is less a mole's-eye view (moles, after all, burrow rather than see) than the awareness that moles, willy-nilly, have an effect. That makes anonymity attractive, but it might not be feasible or responsible. I have to admit that what I deduce is happening contains features that I am happy to see happening, and that what I believe is happening, and will happen, contains features that I believe are beneficial. In the traditional terms of at least one religion, then, I believe it is as important to read the signs of the times as it is hard to kick against the pricks in order to see if they 'be of God'. The naming or identification of these blessings and spirits is a helpful adjunct to thanksgiving (or to exorcism).

Postlude: religion and implicit religion

This three-dimensional model of religiosity has been outlined as a contribution to those concerned with issues in religion (practitioners, leaders and students). Although it is not intended as either another full report (Bailey, 1997a) or another brief introduction (Bailey, 1998b) to implicit religion, the concept has nevertheless cropped up. Partly this is because the model itself was arrived at as a consequence of such study. Indeed, looking back, it was implicit within the original hunch and its first explicit conceptualization. And partly the expression has come into the discussion because it was the original term for the intrinsic religion that was hypothesized as inherently present in contemporary society. (Precision demands a small modification: the original term, in 1967, was 'secular religion': its description as 'implicit religion' dates from 1969.) The development of the model highlighted a potential source of confusion, therefore, and facilitated its clarification.

The first, specific meaning of implicit religion is with reference to contemporary, 'secular' society. It is intended to flag up a heuristic device. The aim is not to prove whether or not it has a religion of its own, which is a semantic question (and so can be side-stepped). The method is to adopt the hypothesis that it has such a religion in order to see whether that enhances our empirical, theoretical and practical understanding of its secularity.

'Implicit religion' was therefore 'defined' in three ways. They were and remain: 'commitment(s)', 'integrating foci' and 'intensive concerns with extensive effects'. The inability to select a single definition (or synonym) at first seemed inadequate but was accepted. Subsequently their plurality seemed to indicate all the more eloquently the reality of that to which they professed to point. Comfort could also have been found in Joachim Wach's constant yet slightly differing definitions of religion (1967). Indeed, any totally satisfying definition of religion would, by definition, not be of *religion*, so a search for a wholly successful definition of *implicit* religion was doubly doomed.

85

As it happened, each of the three definitions (near-synonyms would be more accurate) subsequently turned out to have been particularly appropriate to one of the three empirical contexts that were studied in order to trial the concept. The three contrasting studies were intended to give the results something of the solidity of a tripod. Retrospectively, it was noticed that 'commitments' had been used in the analysis of interviews with individuals; 'integrating foci' had been used to order the report upon the life of the public house; and 'intensive concerns with extensive effects' had provided the summarizing key to the life of the residential community.

Reflection suggests that each of the synonyms places particular emphasis upon at least one of the themes that are intended by the concept of 'implicit religion'. Thus 'commitment' or 'commitments' raises the question whether the religion that is sought is all-embracing or not. It indicates that any commitment is grist to the mill, for consideration as being possibly religious in character; but there is no suggestion that any body has only one commitment (is totally integrated).

'Commitments' also prompts questions as to the level of consciousness that is implied; the degree of deliberateness that is required for behaviour of any kind to qualify as even implicitly religious. The answer of this definition is that religiosity is not to be gauged in either of these ways. It can be present at any level of consciousness: the sub- and un-conscious, the conscious and self-conscious and (what we might term) the sur-conscious. Maslow's 'peak-experiences' are potential evidence; but Schleiermacher's putative dog is not excluded.

'Integrating foci' assumes plurality but prompts the question whether individuals or groups are the subject of investigation. The answer is both (any body). Weber said every group has its own religion; Durkheim would have said it was impossible to be 'a body' without having one. So 'integrating foci' rightly suggests that every conceivable size of sociality should be considered a candidate: the intra- and inter-individual ('personal' is not merely ambiguous but triguous); the social of every degree, the societal of every size, and the species cosmic and corporate.

'Intensive concerns with extensive effects' assumes, after the manner of the social sciences, a multiplicity of commitments or integrating foci, operating within and between the different levels of consciousness and various ranges of sociality. It also assumes, after the manner of East Asian religious practitioners and Japanese religious studies, a multiplicity of objects of commitment or foci of integration. Western religious analysts, by contrast, have deprived themselves of this helpful framework for empirical study. True to their medieval 'Religious' heritage, and ignoring the Semitic vision of all-pervading spiritual warfare, they have preferred to believe that people professing a particular religion possess only that one. However, this synonym also indicates that effect, rather than affect, is crucial to designation as religious.

Drawing up the model placed the specific meaning of the implicit religion of contemporary society (or culture) in context, within a general scheme of religion and consciousness and society. However it highlighted the issue of the relation of implicit religion to religion as a whole.

Explicit religion has always been seen by this student as a possible and proper expression of implicit religion. This, indeed, was one of the reasons for using this expression. (Secular religion suggested that organized religion was not a candidate for inclusion, for whatever reason.) In practise, and in the analysis of practise, often indeed they were impossible to divide. Religion (true or false, boon or bane) served other (secular) ends (even when it regretted doing so). Indeed, when attempting to compile a report upon the residential community of the parish in the form of an exercise in comparative religion, the impossibility of dividing single persons or activities into two religions was confirmed. Conversely (it hardly needs saying), just as explicit religion can express implicit religion, so it can be used for the implicit-religious ends of ulterior motives.

So 'implicit religion', as well as drawing attention to the third type of religiosity, could also be seen as the basis, support or foundation of all three types. Religion, insofar as it was actually religious, whatever the type, was implicit religion made explicit. When challenged to produce a definition of 'implicit religion', it would have been easy to respond, 'When you have produced a definition of religion'. It was tempting to say that implicit religion was religion (Bailey, 1997c) whenever it was really religious (in the sense of being *truly religious*, of course, not in the sense of being *the true* religion).

The heuristic acceptance of both these hypotheses (that secularity has its own implicit religion and that religion *ipso facto* implies religiosity) requires the further development of the model. If 'religion' is to be restricted to the historical type, how are its contemporary and the small-scale equivalents to be described? 'Spirituality' might describe what is present in contemporary culture but what describes what is present in ecological societies? That question in turn raises the fascinating issue of the difference(s) between contemporary spirituality and such archaic spiritualities. That the model provokes such questions must be counted a gain.

The other question must be the linguistic labels 'implicit' and 'explicit' religion. To some extent the problem is solved by the simultaneous use of religiosity (or faith) and religion (or organized religion). (To separate 'tradition' from 'faith' may be seen as 'ideological'.) However, 'spirituality' is in danger of falling into the same trap as 'implicit religion', through being asked to describe both type three religiosity and the inner religion of all three types. Outside the model, it encounters the same problem in being asked to describe both the inner character of a general situation (as in the 'spirituality of a school') where the emphasis is definitely holistic, and at the same time being asked to describe specific means for the attainment of that end (as, usually but not inevitably, in 'spiritual education' or 'spiritual health care').

So these questions, and no doubt many others, remain. They may suggest that the model at least pertains to reality.

6. Some applications

Prelude: a working model?

A conceptual model, if it is to succeed as an item of public property, should meet its owners' mental and practical needs as well as its maker's. So far those needs have been discussed in terms of some of the problems of three groups (the practitioners, leaders and students of religion), of some of their reactions to those problems and of some possible alternative responses to them. As the model arises from consideration of such issues, it was hoped that they would provide a backcloth which would place, contextualize and give some substance to the terms with which it was constructed. It is, however, intended to be a working model: hence the constant desire to speak of, about, to and for both practitioners, leaders and students (most of whom probably occupy two of those categories, if not all three). Perhaps the best test of its functioning as intended is to apply it in situations which were not necessarily part of its original foundation and did not provide the materials for its construction.

The personal settings, from the point of view of social development, have already been described in terms of small-scale ecology, historical society and contemporary culture. Their biographical counterparts are here encapsulated in terms of the cot, the school and the city, and their daily counterparts in terms of the home, the work-team and the airport. The changing character of personal relationships is now illustrated by the varying forms of address: from 'Darling', through 'John', to a number.

The development of general consciousness has likewise been described, along with the concomitant stages of 'religious' (or spiritual) experience. These are illustrated here by their characteristic forms of religious expression: fearing the divine (or shame), praising a personal God ('O God') (or guilt), and joining with a fundamentally, but not ultimately, unknowable GOD (or depression).

Thus the components of the model change from myth-and-ritual, through the Eurocentric religion-and-society, to the current culture-and-spirituality, or, in picture language, from the dew that is all-pervasive but apparent on certain surfaces, through the stage of dazzling clouds in an empty blue sky, to the mist that accompanies a largely unknown Self.

1. Religious: spiritual discernment, religious discrimination and final judgement

Religious Studies is incomplete if it fails to embrace the numerous negativities that religion, as a many-sided phenomenon inculcating bifurcation, inevitably throws up. These will include its direct opposites, such as the belief in no God and disbelief in (or dis-valuation of) religion. They will also include, however, some negativities that are far more significant than these, at least as they are usually understood; for the God that is disbelieved in and the religion that is dismissed are almost always restricted to their historical forms (*a* God, the *organized* religions).

The silence with which religious pastors increasingly seem to respond to confessions of such 'unfaith' may stem from *ennui* with the obsolescence of such non-questions. Manufacturers may react similarly to requests for the rejuvenation of thirty-year-old models of their products, or the comedian's stooge to the question, 'Have you stopped beating your wife yet?'

The 'negativities' which require inclusion in any complete study of religion, across (say) a local area or within a country, are of two sorts. First, there are those phenomena which 'right-thinking' religion prefers to define as outside its remit: what it calls superstition and magic. (Idolatry and paganism used to fall into this category, until the former was spiritualized, and the latter was sanitized.) Unfortunately, the difficulty in agreeing the criteria for 'right thinking' became a reason for their omission rather than for scintillating debate. However, the difficulty of retaining images of belief and ritual as 'pure', when superstition and magic are always so close and so variably intertwined, has been an even more effective reason for their exclusion. They are not simply the other side of the coin; each is intermixed, on both sides of the coin.

The second 'positive' sort of negativity is even more significant: what people positively *dis*believe in (rather than what they *fail* to believe in). These are anti-beliefs, objects of negative faith; what they, often morally, disbelieve *in* rather than merely disbelieve *that*. The Devil, at least in Britain, is hardly likely to come into play here (despite questionnaires that still seem to take medieval Passion Plays as expressive of current, popular metaphysics).

Typically such beliefs are introduced with quiet and apparently humble statements such as, 'I know it's only my opinion, but ...'. They then go on to expound a long-standing, strongly held belief, which is deeply revealing of themselves and which 'wild horses won't make [them] change'. (Hence the quiet confidence of the introduction.) The most frequent examples from the interviews quoted above were 'putting people into categories', 'discrimination' on grounds of race or religion, and 'ticking you off in front of other people'.

Such evidence of where people 'stand' or 'are at', as it is now often expressed, is far too valuable to be ignored. For, on the one hand, although negatives can be ineffable and 'leave [people] speechless', they are far easier to describe, especially to a stranger, than positives. On the other hand, both religion and religious studies have long realized that taboos are signposts pointing negatively towards positive sacreds.

None of these three kinds of negatives (disbelief, superstition, protest) is simply a question for religious studies, however. They are also religious issues. Unbelief may receive philosophical or religious-studies expression but it usually has a pastoral undertow, a basis in personal experience. Belief or behaviour that is considered marginally or dangerously religious is an invitation to pastoral care, wherever it occurs. Anti-beliefs, if shared, are often the springs of redemptive action.

However, they all pose a problem for religion and, indirectly, for religious studies. It was foreshadowed, as it happens, in one of the anti-beliefs quoted. If the drawing of distinctions is an inevitable result in consciousness of the development of religiosity, and if its evaluative aspect is successfully disciplined (in the interests of morality as well as practicality), how is it possible to restore these repressed aspects of identity and integrity, and to rank what has been distinguished?

Must liberality forever conceal its convictions as to the negative half of the truth as perceived and be content to be overriden? The Christian injunction was to '*turn* the other cheek' and offer it for hitting (a provocative act), not to be a silent, passive walkover. This is, perhaps, today's religious issue *par excellence*.

Any guidance that is offered, must steer a 'middle path' between the 'fundamentalist' simplicity of a pocket generality such as, 'Love your neighbour as yourself', and the 'casuistic' complexities of context-bound relevances, such as the legalized taboos of Leviticus or caste. What is required is a methodology for personal decision-making. Three steps may be involved.

The first is the need for spiritual discernment. The concern is with motive or, better, spirit, although consequence (and public effect) will not be ignored. If, tongue half in cheek, ten easy steps to such discernment were to be formulated, they might run as follows (where 'it' refers to *any* 'body', whether composed of a single individual or of a multiplicity of members):

Does it *say* it stands for anything?
If so, what does the body mean by it?

Does it use any *non-verbal* symbols of itself in communicating with itself or others?
If so, why does it use these particular symbols?

What else seems to be typical of or significant about the body?
What do they reveal about its intentions?

What does the body keep silent in the face of or about?
What do the silences say?

What does the body hope for?
How does it expect it to come about?

An alternative decalogue of methodological questions might run:

How does it believe life is? and might be?
What does it feel must be done? and not done?
Who does it have solidarity with? and who not?
What brings it to life? and what does it abhor?
Who is it? and who is it not?

The second step must be one of *proper* 'religious discrimination', that is to say, based upon spiritual discernment, not taking short-cuts through the use of quick and slick 'party labels'. A ten-step guide might run:

What is the spirit of the activity, institution, etc.?
Is it a religious issue or a theological, ethical, moral, aesthetic, cultural or social one?

In what ways does, and doesn't, the phenomenon match its profession? Is it spiritually self-aware?

Is it self-critical?
Is it capable of entering into dialogue?

Is it concerned for truth more than for itself?
Is the spirit capable of growth?

Is it capable of encouraging growth in others?
Is its spirit (in Christian terms) Holy?

The third step involves a double recognition. First, we cannot become fully human without every day making such judgements (discerning and discriminating) as are involved in setting goals and prioritizing. Second, that our judgements reveal our selves most clearly, so that by our own judgements we ourselves are and shall be judged, whoever our various judges.

2. Spiritual: coinherence and intercession, adoration and confession, contemplation and worship

Biblically the Spirit (above all, with the capital letter), like the Kingdom, is described by metaphor or illustrated by example rather than defined. The impossibility of defining either Spirit or Kingdom would seem to be inherent in the phenomena to which the terms point. As these phenomena in some way or other must be central to religion (whatever form religion takes), this would seem to be one reason, among others, for the inherent impossibility of defining religion definitively.

Yet the definition, description, meaning or criteria of spiritual and spirituality is a matter of practical, pastoral concern. Since the remarkable 'return' to popular acceptability of those concepts around 1980, the rejuvenation of the spiritual among the aims of British education by the government later in that decade, and its introduction into the aims of healthcare (in the wake of the hospice movement), educational and health workers have become increasingly monitored upon their provision for a spiritual dimension.

Unfortunately there is confusion (or worse) as to what they are even expected to do, let alone how it will be judged or people trained to do it. In view of the extra strain that is inevitably involved in being assessed on work of a personal kind, to be judged on what is of particular sensitivity but otherwise a blank sheet of paper, results in problems of a pastoral nature among the staff, let alone the deprivation of their charges and clients.

Western cultural history can offer two strands towards the understanding of spirit. The first may be associated with Ancient Greece and would see the spirit as inherent within a person. It is that which distinguishes a living human being from 'their' dead body, whose departure changes the corporately animate into the inanimate corpse. By extension it becomes possible to speak of the 'genius' of a place or of other apparently inanimate things. The emphasis is upon life as individually distinctive.

The second strand is Hebraic. Biblically, the spirit, or perhaps better the Spirit, is that which joins things together by going between them. The emphasis is upon life through mutuality. Putting the two approaches together, we can see the spirit as that which dwells within and reaches out or as that which enlivens each by uniting both (an opinion, incidentally, with which the interviewees would have agreed).

Closely linked with the question of meaning, for practitioners, leaders and analysts in the field of spiritual education and spiritual care, is the question of methodology. Is spirituality a separate activity or a dimension of every activity? Or is there a 'middle path' again between those two ends of the spectrum, as predicated perhaps by worship and religious education in schools, and by prayers and the provision of chapels and chaplains in hospitals? Does the widening of that special, dedicated and focused provision, into the additional provision of counselling in both schools and hospitals, meet the stated need? Can the spiritual be catered for by the provision of opportunity for relating with Divinity liturgically, and by provision of food for the mind, balm for the emotions, strength for the will and a human and physical environment in which the person can flourish? Is it more than the sum of such parts or are such 'parts' themselves, in fact, aspects of that whole?

Perhaps the answer should be neither the one nor the other, but 'both ... and'. For it is dependent on the nature of human being, and human being is both a system which is more than the sum of its parts (the spirit can be given up) and yet is dependent on its parts, if it is to survive. So the education or the health of a human can be divided up or broken down and, yet, can be distinguished from all such division and can survive virtually complete break-down of the parts. The child can grow in wisdom, for instance, through that interaction with things (not least, the self) that the passage of time brings about, and the patient who is sore afflicted and helpless can still aver, 'But I'm all right in myself, you know', and one does. Perhaps the one thing that alone is needful, on the part of those with responsibility for these things, is a self-awareness. Monitoring stimulates such corporate self-criticism and self-improvement by focusing and symbolizing the need for such procedures.

Charities in Britain are now required to preface their accounts with an annual estimate of the extent to which they have achieved their goals. So every local church has to produce a Mission Statement against which to judge itself (a double irony). Were they to be monitored for their spirituality, some interesting feathers might fly; yet many a visitor does precisely this (as parents visit schools), before choosing which one to join. Their 'instinct' (culturally formed by two millennia of penetration) is sound: the church exists as a spiritual body (whose spirit, hopefully, is the spirit of its professed Divinity), whose observable activities are signs of its life (for good or ill).

It is possible that, just as the visitor is often both discerning and discriminating, in knowing what to look for and how to find it, so such a specialist institution, and other religions, have some particular contribution to offer to the general weal on the subject of the spiritual. One such contribution might be teaching on coinherence. It is beautifully portrayed in the picture of the three 'persons' (cp. the *masks* worn by the *dramatis personae* in classical drama) of the Trinity as 'mutually indwelling'. The doctrine (echoed by John Donne) says that human beings likewise live 'in' one another. (A grandmother in the interviews said she mostly lived 'through' her family now.) It may be obvious to any parent or lover (and applied by Paul to the Christian and Christ) but popular versions of the social sciences still tend to think in terms of models based on atomized individuals organized into systems. Children, moved to intercession by the plight of refugees (or of rabbits), experiencing the sacred as identification and integration 'with', and those other wets and softies, who are moved by the Spirit to pity or prayer, have a particular contribution to make in this area.

Another such contribution could be made by Evangelicals who 'love the Lord'; by teenagers in the throes of passionate ('suffering') love; and by neurotic seekers after relationships. For these people, once they have moved beyond the initial, mutual 'possession', may experience the other as adorable or holy, whom (for the sake of *both*) they 'would fain not offend', but to whom they know they can confess the truth of both their love and their inadequacy, knowing that each of them is believed and forgiven ('accepted', but positively so – 'welcomed').

A third contribution could be made by the agnostic, the Buddhist, the artist, the adult whose faith has 'grown out of' the highly personal, the one who cannot but see the cosmos as a system, the one who is committed to the human as a whole being, body, warts and all. Their contribution is contemplative: to give the parts and the whole the opportunity to be themselves with us, to communicate themselves, to 'speak for themselves', to be heard for what they are. Their calling is to put the 'th' back into *wor'ship*, so that to 'worship you with my body' no longer sounds blasphemous or 'his Worship the Mayor' ludicrous, and 'wor(th)ship' is of divinity wherever it be found, without its having to be restricted to a singular, 'personal' Deity.

3. Human: growing, doing, dying

'Religion represents life at its most intense', said Stanley Cook in his great article on religion (1918). His account then went on to differ from Durkheim. Cook said it was unlikely people would ever agree on a common definition of religion, until they could agree on a common definition of life (meaning life in a qualitative sense with an initial capital letter, Life). Durkheim thought (or hoped or assumed) we had a common understanding of religion because we had a common understanding of the sacred. But he did not explicitly associate the 'life' which he found in all social 'as-sociat-ions' with the religious, in the way that Cook would have done.

Durkheim, as a Jewish contemporary of Dreyfus, was fighting for the autonomy of secularity; Cook was living in a (non-militantly but officially) religious community in Cambridge, England. For him, the sacred was perhaps less that which is special because *set apart* from the secular (the rest of life) than that which is special because *central* to the whole of life.

96

The difference may be illustrated by the ambiguity of 'apart'. Durkheim, had he written in English, would have used 'apart' to mean 'aside' (and anticipated that what was once 'a side' of life, as a whole, could now, in the form of religion, be set on one side or aside). Cook, on the other hand, would have used 'apart' to mean 'a part', albeit a 'vital' part, of life.

The application of this 'three-dimensional' model to 'life', as distinct from 'religion' or 'spirituality', is therefore difficult but semantically rather than conceptually or practically. The confusion arises from the multiplicity of uses to which 'religion' has been put. In terms of this model, it has been projected backwards from its religion-and-society context on to the myth/ritual-and-ecology situation, which it only just fits. Because it has often been equated with the sacred, it has also been assumed that 'it' could (or could not) be similarly projected forwards on to the spirituality-and-culture context. The answer to this is that it can and it cannot. On the one hand, historical-type religions and religiosity survive and to some extent thrive within contemporary culture; so do the concept and practises of 'spirituality'. On the other hand, that which is *distinctive* of contemporary spirituality is different from that which is *distinctive* of historical religion, in the recent past or the present.

In practice, this causes little difficulty. Being religious has always meant a way of life centred upon a chosen core. The man-in-the-street ('person-on-the-pavement'?) says, 'I read the papers religiously', meaning: regularly (as though according to a *Regula*, Rule) but not automatically (as though obeying the inevitability of biological need or psychological compulsion); habitually but by choice (a habit is worn deliberately to signify one's 'profession'); consciously and conscientiously but without any suggestion that this is a rationality or morality that is for all. Indeed, the same person-on-the-pavement demonstrates his/her understanding of the word precisely, when saying, for instance: 'She goes to church every week, but her real religion is [her children, gossiping or whatever].' They are then conducting an exercise in *comparative* religion.

The similarity with the Benedictine use of *religio* is remarkable. It may be peculiar to English English. However, English society, culture, religion and spirituality have been described as continuing to be Benedictine in tone: local but holistic (as in the civil and ecclesiastical parish system, as in the school system until the centralization of the 1980s, and as in medical 'general practice');

social rather than communal, respecting authority rather than self-denying, admiring of 'village Hampden's' and of restraint in rulers. Whatever may have been the case in eighteenth or nineteenth century France, there is no need to posit the suggestion that *religio* on this side of the Channel, in ordinary speech, was derived from classical Latin: the medieval usage is closer to today's and historically much more likely to be its source.

Religion, in its 'historical' form, makes sense in intellectual contexts along with its counterparts, 'secular' and 'society' (in the systemic, sociological sense). Non-intellectuals can understand what is meant in that context, but the intelligentsia sometimes forget how limited that context is, in proportion to society as a whole. It would be a rare lecturer in sociology or social anthropology who would think of introducing the concepts of 'society' and 'culture' by even mentioning their earlier, non-systemic, model-type use, as in the expressions '(high) Society' or '(normative) Culture'.

Typically, for instance, the governing body of a school or the teaching staff will express surprise at the description of the rest of the curriculum apart from Religious Education as 'secular'. They laugh, indeed, not only because it is obvious and 'ordinary' (what school is for and life is about), but because anyone thought of labelling it at all, especially in that way. They are amused, not by any particular valuation but by the division. They assume the whole curriculum (apart perhaps from Religious Education) is secular and yet is somehow expressive of a core and so, simultaneously, religious. Perhaps the division only makes sense when children are seen primarily in terms of what they will become (and when the distinctive element of 'will' is overlooked in such predictions, 'shall' being intended).

The sudden return of 'the spiritual' to acceptability and its immediate rise almost to the status of fashionability, about 1980, cannot have been without significance for the student (or, indeed, the leader or the practitioner) of religion. It marked a complete about-turn on the situation prevailing formerly. At a conference of serious, high-minded and idealistic schoolteachers in 1966, for instance, the tension became dramatic when some members at the organization's annual meeting wanted to include 'spiritual' among their corporate aims. (They were mainly females, aged about 50, and sounded as though they could have been members of the Society of Friends.) The suggestion was opposed (significantly, mainly by males aged about

40) on the repeated grounds that the concept was both incomprehensible and yet somehow dangerous (because opening the door to 'religion').

However, by 1980 society at large (including young males, in the newer sectors of employment such as computing and finance) found meaning, without menace, in the word. For them, religion no more had a monopoly of the spiritual than (after about 1970) it had of the pastoral (or, after about 1990, of ritual); indeed, spirituality was often not even associated with religion. In the same way, religion was less often seen, even by the intellectuals who followed the old model, as the enemy of the secular, or the secular as the opposite of religion, while 'materialism', which religious leaders had diabolized, seemed to disappear from their diatribes a couple of decades before the collapse of Communism in 1989.

One of the issues facing the religions is how to re-present themselves as a dimension of life at large, as the focus of life at its most intense, as Life in a qualitative sense, and yet retain their communal base and material infrastructure. The spiritual experience they enshrine (especially when they are willing to listen, sift and incorporate 'the wisdom of the simple'), and the explicit spiritual teaching in their traditions, are *sans pareil* and its communication can be economically viable but it does not necessarily lead to increased membership and, indeed, such sharing is difficult to combine with recruitment.

New institutions may have been arising without religious affiliation since 1600 (Greeley, 1973), but since 1700 an ever-increasing number of Christian (rather than Church) organizations have been established, first as para-Church groups and then as philanthropic organizations in which religious and secular-minded people could cooperate without argument. As the monastic Orders were, first, spontaneous and local, then unified and Papal and finally uneasily related to dioceses, so these 'religious orders' were, first, spontaneous but national, then uneasily related to denominations and, finally, increasingly free-floating.

The nub of the problem for religion, at least in its Western-Christian form, however, might well be a certain lack of sheer vitalism, epitomized in the vitality of virility. It is impossible to redeem before embracing the energy of youth, the creativity emancipated by equality, the knowledge and critical faculty facilitated by education, the time freed for spiritual development by increased health and longevity, and the call for discernment and discrimination necessitated by plurality. This cannot be achieved in the medieval mission-station manner, by setting up holistic nuclei or totalitarian institutions. Effort must be focused into specialized but significant contributions. Among these must be religion itself and spirituality (the form taken by religiosity in contemporary culture).

In this area, for instance, the religions can challenge their recent, mutually exclusive compartmentalization by scholars, as much as by their own leaders, and can insist upon a pluralism that goes beyond the coexistence of mere tolerance towards a plurality which recognizes selective syncretism as a normal and inevitable process, in the canon and the populace alike. When such realities and ideals are welcomed, then each is free to offer their own unique contribution.

Another sphere in which Western-Christian religion, at least, is failing to share some of its traditional heritage is in the area that was once known as 'growing old gracefully'. The emphasis upon activity has been highly productive; but the proportion of each of the four Gospels given over to the account of Christ's climactic change from a doing ministry to a suffering one suggests that the reaction against the fatalism of Catholic popular religion and the servility of Protestant nineteenth-century religion in turn needs redressing. Most attention may inevitably be given to change, but most of life (gender, parentage, mother tongue, ethnic group and so on) is rarely subject to change. Spirituality is as present in these spheres as in any other: religions need to be relevant in such situations again.

Postlude

This volume has tried to set in order a number of thoughts. First it has not wanted to separate the practitioner of religion from the leader or the student of religion. Rightly or wrongly it believes they are often three faces of the one person today. Even if they are not, it is believed that they need to communicate with each other more than they seem able to do at present.

Second it has talked of recent and current issues in religion by concentrating upon the 'religious' element. This has been seen not in terms of theology, historical causes and effects, or changes in the symbolic systems of liturgy and scripture, but in terms of 'religious' motivations. These have been gauged by what people are committed to and what brings them to life or Life (and so, of what they might be prepared to die for).

Possible alternative responses for practitioners, leaders and students alike have also been outlined. This allowed changes from inherited patterns, whose motivation can be underestimated by both supporters and opponents of tradition alike, to be given the opportunity of a religious rather than secular interpretation. Those who would spurn a 'high society' or 'high culture' (Society or Culture with the capital initial letter) approach, sometimes enjoy unity in adopting a 'high Religion' attitude, using pretended humour as a cover for actual mockery.

A three-dimensional model of 'religiosity' (what makes 'religion' religious) was then described. It speaks of sensing the sacred, encountering the holy and commitment to the human. The first type of religious experience was seen as characteristic of small-scale 'ecology'-type societies, whether tribal or infantile or intimate, in which consciousness intensifies and then splits, centring positively (and negatively) upon the sacred and profane (or negatively sacred). The second type was seen as characteristic of 'historical' societies, whether in the traditional city or among teenagers or in work-teams, in which individuation gives opportunity for interrelationship and the sacred becomes focused in a more religious holy, which is 'encountered' rather than 'sensed'. The third type of religious experience characterizes life in contemporary culture, whether crowded or lonely, in which consciousness becomes both highly conscious of itself and of its context, and the holy is diffused, again, but this time mainly at the human level, to which selves commit themselves.

If only in the belief that the consideration of issues in religion calls for transparency and humanity, an attempt was made to 'extrapolate' this model by consideration of the current appeal of the concepts of 'integrity' and 'identity', and the possibilities that the rehabilitation of 'Divinity' might offer. Then, following the Religious Studies principle that every negative points to a positive, it was considered 'evitable' that such an 'extrapolation' might be balanced by an 'intrapolation', confirming that rockets are launched from pads built on sand. The concluding Applications of this

101

understanding of religion inevitably run the gauntlet between the stratosphere and the concrete, the human and the humane, but again it is hoped that each aspect can illuminate the others and some new ways might have been suggested.

Appendix
Spirituality, religion and consciousness:
a developmental model

IDENTITY

Human environment	General consciousness	Personalities	Spiritual experience	Religious expression	Conceptual metaphor
Small-scale ecology	Intensification and bifurcation	Knee Home	A sense of the sacred	Fear 'The Divine'	Myth/ritual: Dew
Historical society	Individuation and interrelationship	School Group	An encounter with the Holy	Praise 'O God'	Society/religion: Clouds
Contemporary culture	Conscientization and contextualization	City Community	Commitment to the human	Join 'GOD'	Culture/spirituality: Mist

INTEGRITY

Bibliography

Badertscher, J. (2002), 'The centrality of the concept of implicit religion for Religious Studies', in E. I. Bailey (ed.), *Papers in Implicit Religion*. Lampeter, Wales: Edwin Mellen Press.

Bailey, E. I. (1969), 'The Religion of a "Secular" Society', M.A. thesis, Bristol University Library.

Bailey, E. I. (1976), 'Emergent Mandalas: The Implicit Religion of Contemporary Society', Ph.D. thesis, University of Bristol (catalogued as 'The Religion of a Secular Society').

Bailey, E. I. (1990a), 'The "implicit religion" concept as a tool for ministry', *Sociological Focus*, 23(3): 203–17, Bowling Green State University, Ohio, Department of Sociology.

Bailey, E. I. (1990b), 'Common religion in context: the suburb', paper at St George's House Consultation, Windsor Castle, pp. 21–3.

Bailey, E. I. (1995), 'Let's listen to the natives', *Journal for the Scientific Study of Religion*, 34(3): 391–2.

Bailey, E. I. (1997a), *Implicit Religion in Contemporary Society*. Kampen, Netherlands: Kok Pharos.

Bailey, E. I. (1997b), 'The popular religion of a secular society', paper presented at conference at The Open University, Milton Keynes.

Bailey, E. I. (1997c), 'Religion and implicit religion: which is the analogy?' *Modern Believing*, (NS) 38(2): 30–6.

Bailey, E. I. (1998a), 'Soviet and Western introductions to the study of religion: a bibliography', *Reconciliation: Journal of Reconciliation*: 28–32.

Bailey, E. I. (1998b), *Implicit Religion: An Introduction*. London: Middlesex University Press.

Bailey, E. I. (ed.) (1998–) *Implicit Religion: Journal of the Centre for the Study of Implicit Religion and Contemporary Spirituality*, Leeds: Maney and Co.

Bailey, E. I. (2000), 'The sacred, the holy, and the human, as tripartite symbols of Ultimate Reality and Meaning', *Ultimate Reality and Meaning*, 22(3).

Banham, D. (1991), *Monasteriales Indicia: The Anglo-Saxon Monastic Sign Language*. Middlesex, Anglo-Saxon Books.

Barry, S. J. (1997), *'Our Way of Proceeding'*: *To Make the Constitutions of the Society of Jesus and Their Complementary Norms Our Own*. St Louis, MO: The Institute of Jesuit Sources.

Baum, G. (1975), *Religion and Alienation: A Theological Reading of Sociology*. New York: Paulist Press.

Bouquet, A. C. (1954), *Comparative Religion: A Short Outline*. Harmondsworth: Penguin.

Bromley, D. and Greil, A. L. (eds) (forthcoming), *Defining Religion*. Greenwich, CT: JAI Press.

Cantwell Smith, W. (1964), *The Meaning and End of Religion*. New York: Macmillan.

Cook, S. A. (1918), 'Religion', *Encyclopaedia of Religion and Ethics*, Vol. X: 662–93, J. Hastings (ed.), Edinburgh: T. and T. Clark.

Cox, H. (1965), *The Secular City: Secularization and Urbanisation in Theological Perspective*. London: SCM Press.

Davie, G. (1990), 'Believing without belonging: is this the future of religion in Britain?' paper at St George's House Consultation, Windsor Castle.

Dicey, A. V. (1893), *Law and Opinion in England in the Nineteenth Century*. Edinburgh: R. and R. Clark.

Dupré, W. (2002), 'The Priority of the Holy: some remarks of the distinction between the sacred and the holy', in E. I. Bailey (ed.), *Denton Papers in Implicit Religion*. Lampeter: Edwin Mellen Press.

Durkheim, E. (1947), *The Elementary Forms of the Religious Life*, trans. S. W. Swain, Glencoe, IL: Free Press.

Edwards, D. L. (1969), *Religion and Change*. London: Hodder and Stoughton.

Grainger, R. B. (2001), 'The implicit religion of King Lear', paper at 23rd Denton Conference in Implicit Religion, 5–7 May, expected in *Implicit Religion*, 4, Leeds: Maney and Co.

Greeley, A. (1973), *The Persistence of Religion*. London: SCM Press.

Hay, D. (1982), *Exploring Inner Space: Scientists and Religious Experience*. Harmondsworth: Penguin.

James, W. [1902] (1960), *The Varieties of Religious Experience: A Study in Human Nature*. London: Collins.

Jenkins, T. (1999), *Religion in English Everyday Life: An Ethnographic Approach*. Oxford: Bergholm Books.

Journal of Oriental Studies 26(1), (1987), 'Beyond the dichotomy of secularity and religion'. Tokyo: Institute of Oriental Philosophy.

106

Luckmann, T. (1967), *The Invisible Religion: The Problem of Religion in Modern Society*. London: Collier-Macmillan.

Martin, D. (1968), 'City Man II', in *Frontier*, 11(1), Spring. London: Dominion Press.

Martin, D. (1969), *The Religious and the Secular*. London: Routledge and Kegan Paul.

Martin, D. (1973), 'The secularization question', in *Theology*, February. London: SPCK.

Marty, M. E. (1975), *A Nation of Behavers*. Chicago: University of Chicago Press.

Ménard, G. (ed.) (1990–), *Religiologiques*. Montréal: Université de Québec.

Moore, S. F. and Myerhoff, B. G. (eds) (1977), *Secular Ritual*. Amsterdam: Van Gorcum.

Oman, J. (1931), *The Natural and the Supernatural*. Cambridge: Cambridge University Press.

Panikkar, R. (1978), 'Time and sacrifice: the sacrifice of time and the ritual of modernity', *The Study of Time*, III, *Proceedings of the Third Conference of the International Society for the Study of Time*, D. Park, N. Lawrence and J. T. Fraser (eds), New York: Springer-Verlag.

Srinivas, M. N. (1952), *Religion and Society among the Coorgs of South India*. London: J. K. Publishers.

Stanner, W. E. H. (1963), 'The dreaming', in T. A. G. Hungerford (ed.), *Australian Signpost*, Melbourne: F. W. Cheshire.

Toynbee, A. J. (1933–9), *A Study of History*, Volumes I–X. London: Oxford University Press.

Toynbee, A. J. (1961), *A Historian Looks at Religion*. London: Oxford University Press.

Waardenburg, J. (1973), *Classical Approaches to the Study of Religion: Aims, Methods and Theories of Research*. The Hague: Mouton.

Wach, J. (1967), *The Sociology of Religion*. Chicago: Chicago University Press.

Watts, I. (1674–1748), 'When I survey the wondrous Cross' (in most English-language Christian hymnaries).

Weber, M. [1904–5] (1930), *The Protestant Ethic and the Spirit of Capitalism*, trans. T. Parsons. London: Unwin.

Welbourn, F. B. (1965), *Religion and Politics in Uganda, 1952–1962*. Nairobi: East Africa Publishing House.

Wilson, M. (1971), *Religion and the Transformation of Society: A Study of Social Change in Africa*. Cambridge: Cambridge University Press.

Index

INDEX

pastoral care   3, 21, 48, 51, 91, 93, 94
personal, the   4, 42, 45, 46, 74, 96
   sacred, holy and   79–80
personhood   3–4, 94–5, 103
pluralism   48, 49, 100
politics and religion   2, 18, 35, 36
popular religion   25, 49
postmodernism   1, 15, 25
power   2, 38
prayer   31, 52, 95
preaching   21, 53
profane, the   57, 58–9, 63, 101
professionalization   65, 77, 84
Protestantism   24, 42, 65, 100
psychology   15, 51, 66
public house study (Bailey)   81, 86

Quakers   56
quantitative research   79–81
   see also interviews and surveys

rationalization   17–18
'real' religion   44
redemption   91
   see also atonement
reductionalism   22
Reformation   16
regula, see religio
relationship   35, 69–70, 72–3, 96
   divine–human   3–4, 89–90
   identity and   82–3
religio (rule of life)   16, 35, 38, 55, 56,
   58, 64, 67, 97–8
religion   19, 42, 63–4, 81, 83, 90
   historical forms of   75, 98
   misunderstanding of   8–10, 11–12,
      13, 46, 53
   nature and function of   13, 39, 43–5,
      52–3, 99
   and secularization   54, 66
   and society   43–4, 49, 60, 67–8, 74,
      87, 97
   vicarious participation in   19, 47
   see also definition of religion; explicit
      religion; organized religion
religiosity   26, 39, 42, 43, 63, 74, 78,
   86–8, 91, 100, 101

and commitment   81, 83
of everyday life   70, 71–3
measuring   9
religious, the   50, 55, 56–7, 78, 80, 83,
   87, 100–1
religious experience   25, 37, 44, 63, 89,
   101, 103
   analysis and morphology of   3–4, 32
   and social experience   70–3
religious leaders   13, 38, 45, 68, 85, 89,
   100
   and religious expression   18–22, 26
   response to contemporary
      situations   36, 47–8, 51–3, 98,
      101
religious practitioners   13, 14–18, 25,
   27, 29, 38, 47–8, 87, 89, 98, 100,
   101
   and religious living   68–9
   self-identification   22, 23, 34–5, 51,
      52
Religious Studies   23–4, 25, 39, 41, 63,
   67, 69–70, 73, 75, 77–8, 90–1,
   101
   see also students of religion
renewal and revivalism   37–8
revelation   26
reverence   24, 25
ritual   17, 36, 68, 97, 103
   and liturgy   38–9, 40, 58
Roman Catholicism   8, 9, 17, 24, 38,
   65, 100
Roman religion   45–6

sacrament   10, 21, 22, 75
sacred, the   3, 24, 78–80, 81, 82–3, 95,
   96, 101, 103
   interface with secular   21, 31–2, 63,
      75
   and profane in Durkheim   57–60
scapegoat   43, 82
Schleiermacher, Friedrich   37, 86
science   42, 45, 78
scripture   17, 24, 36, 101
secular agencies and religious
   initiatives   51–2
secularity   2, 44, 49, 57, 66, 87, 96

112